Ian Charles Scott

The
SHAPE
of the
BEING

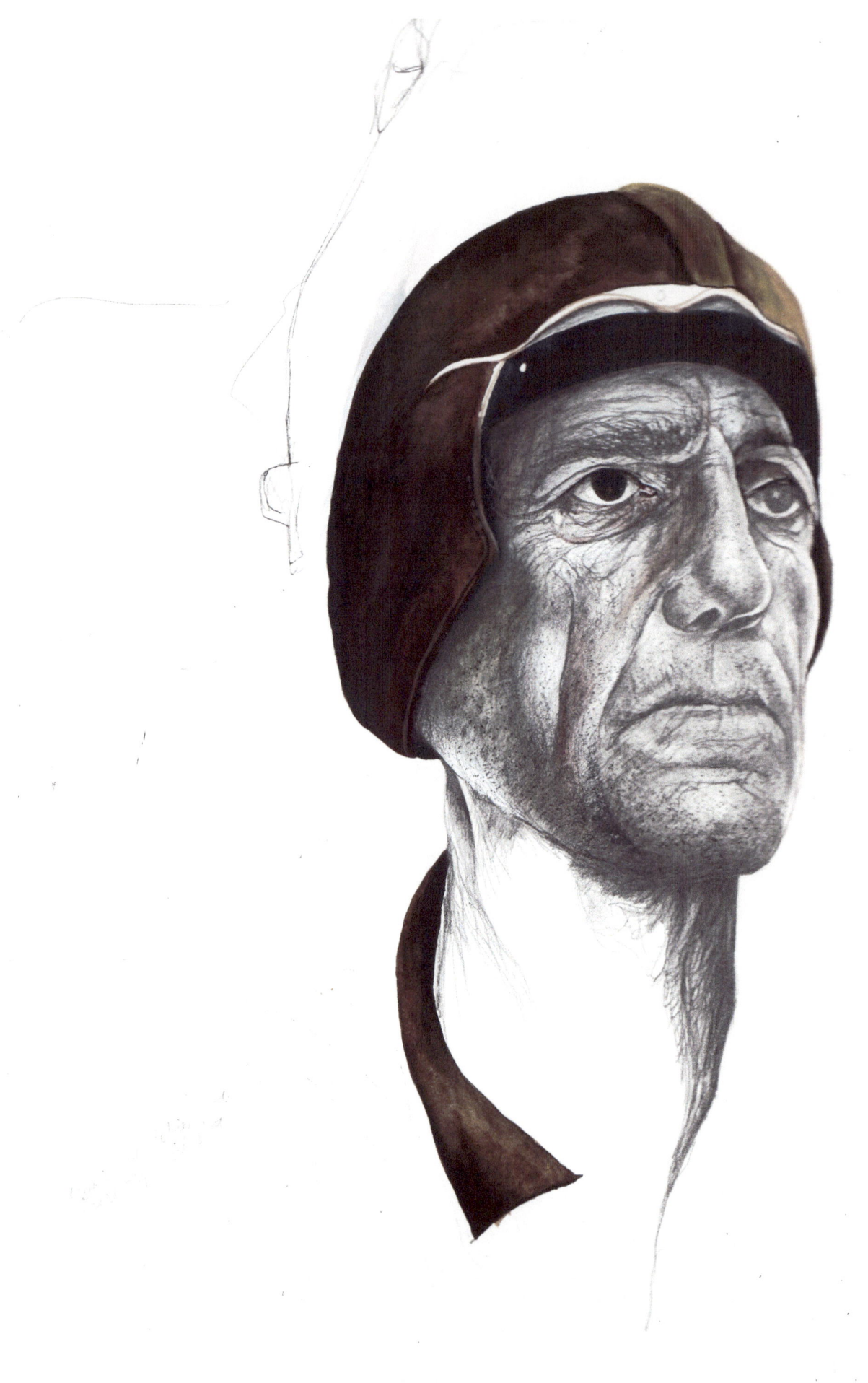

Ian Charles Scott

The
SHAPE
of the
BEING

VICTORY HALL PRESS

Front Cover: The Shape of the Being, 8" x 8", oil on Panel 2014

Frontispiece: Construction Worker, pencil and water colour on paper, 18" x 14" 2013

Opposite: Catch 22 Chelsea, NY, oil on paper, 24" X 18" 2011

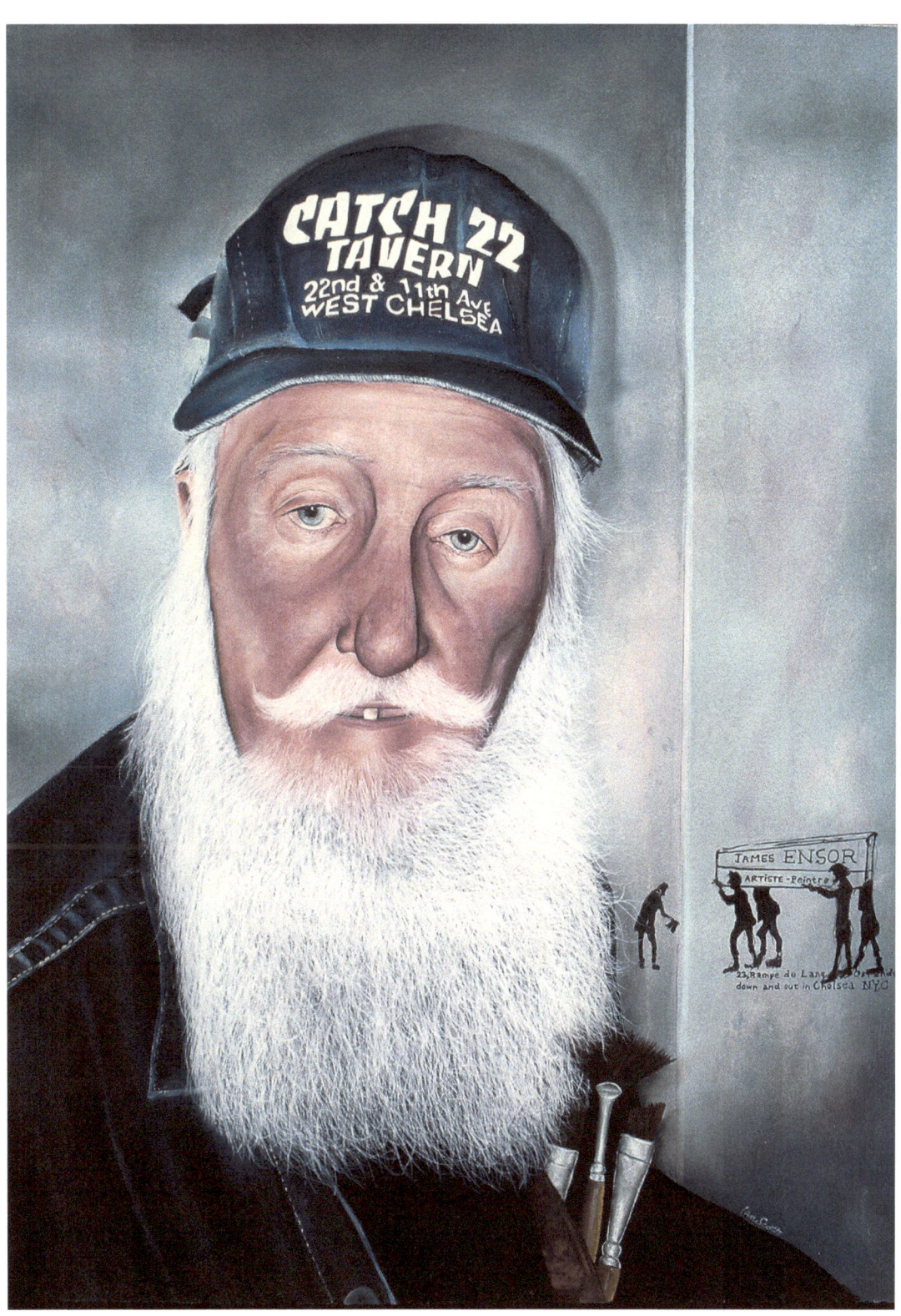

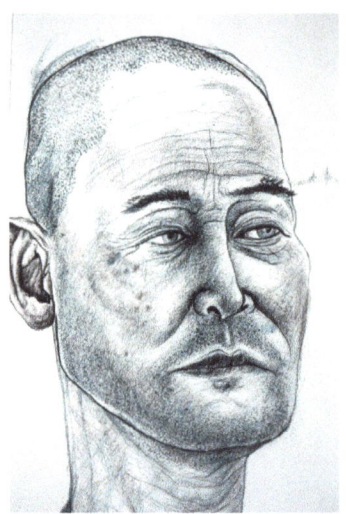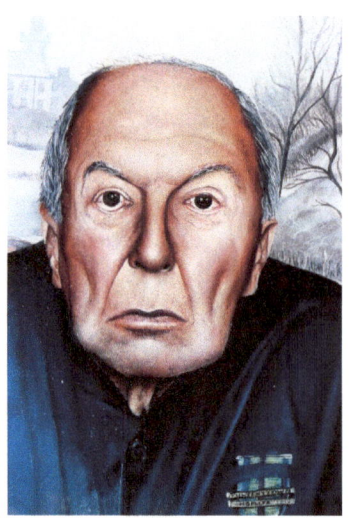

Top- left to right

Sunim, coloured pencil drawing, 10" x 8" 2007

Pulteney Passendale, Oil On Panel, 10"x 8" 2009

George In Braemore, watercolours, 10" x 8" 2003

Tweedie paints at home, oil on panel, 9" x 12" 2003

Harbourmaster's Office, oil on panel, 18" x 24" 2005

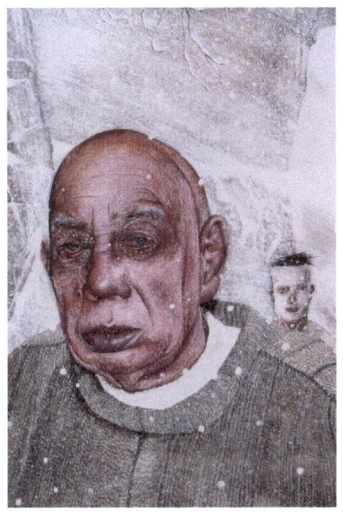 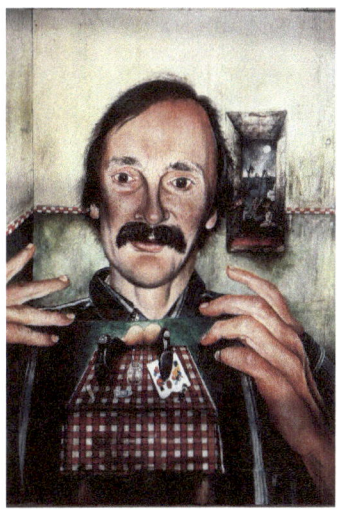 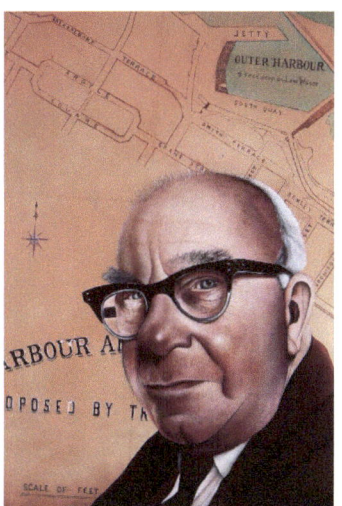

Ian Charles Scott's Portraits: An Introduction

For Ian Charles Scott, New York City seems only a larger version of the community he knew in his Scottish hometown of Wick - a bigger village. As a professor at Hostos College in the Bronx, he brings an energy and dedication to his interactions with the people he serves. This same sense of engagement with those around him leads him to investigate what he refers to as "the shape of the being"- the nature of humanity, and serves him as he seeks out subjects for his paintings.

They tend to be men on both ends of life's spectrum, the special as well as the unusual. He finds them in the interesting characters that inhabit his northern coast-town of Wick, his new hometown in the Bronx, or the Chelsea gallery area of Manhattan. He has also sought out as subjects for his work, men of character and note from his native land as well as from his new one. He is fascinated by them all and presents them all with understanding and dignity. His intense interest makes for an equally intense, vibrant portrait.

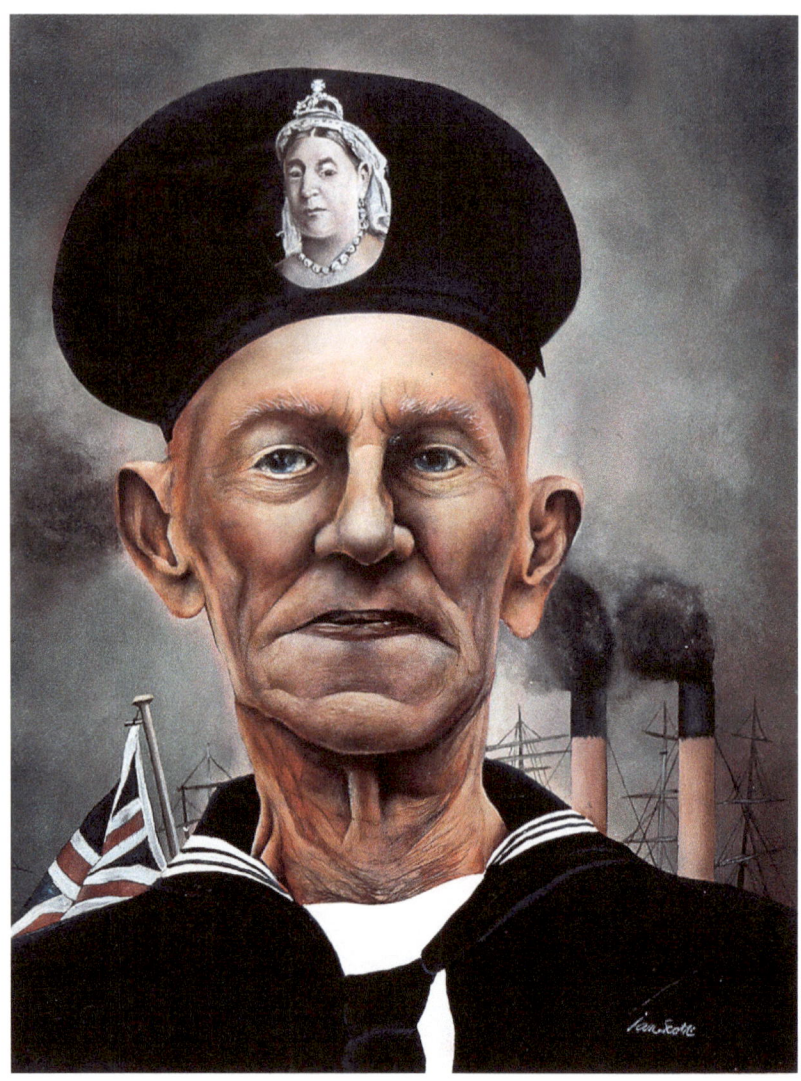

Victory At Sea, oil on panel 10" X 8" 2007

Scott's artistic output takes two forms. Some of his paintings are wildly imaginative tableaus of people he has known in fantastic situations. Of these he claims, 'everything I paint could actually happen in reality'. These will be the subjects of a companion volume to this one. Then there are the more straightforward portraits. These are no less dramatic, in many ways even more so, than the scenes. These are not portraits for commission. They are made to please the artist, not the sitter.

Scott's drive for painting these people seems to be to study them, to perceive something about their inner nature. These are in many ways psychological studies of men he admires as well as men he finds puzzling, has compassion for but finds hard to understand in some ways. At the least, they are very different men than he, living very different lives. Perhaps he sees their lives as alternate possibilities for his own and wonders how one man gets to be one way and another quite different.

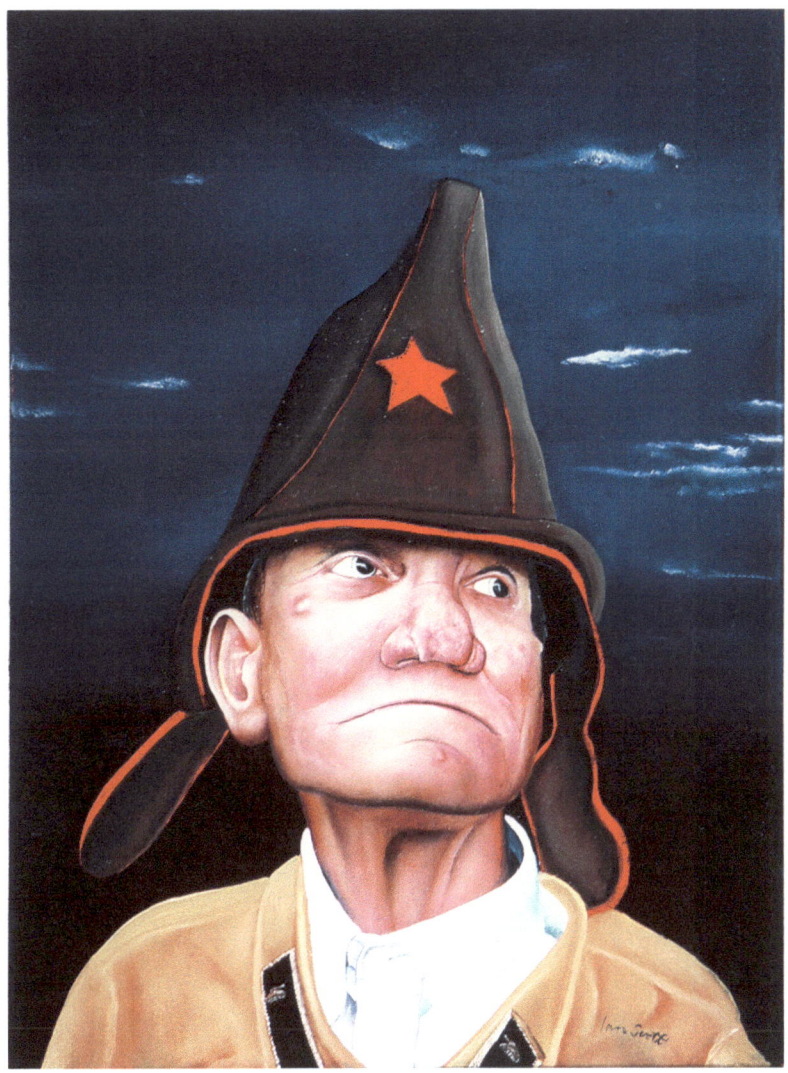

The Russian, 10" x 8" oil on panel 2009

For Scott, the artist's role is to record and study-to show forth the reality we see and the reality we must look deeper for. This is why these portraits, are both compelling and at times repelling, and why they have something special to communicate to us.

The works in this book cover the whole of Ian Scott's career and divide into distinct groupings. There are the recent images that we see on these pages of familiar faces from both cities: the Catch-22 man Scott stopped coming out of a James Ensor exhibition in New York, and the harbormaster, old sailor, and postmaster of Wick. The current, ink pictures of boxers and other Bronx and Brooklyn neighbors are remarkable for their piercing gaze and clarity of color. Sections on Scott's studies of a few notable men follow, concluding with several very large, powerful works on wood panel that helped start-off his career, and all of which are in the collections of various Scottish museums.

- James Pustorino,

Editor

Bronx Boxers and other New York Ink Portraits

2011-12

Based on boxers from a gym near Hostos College, former next-door neighbors in Brooklyn and others Scott has come across.

Bronx Boxer

ink, watercolours and gouache on paper

12" x 9"

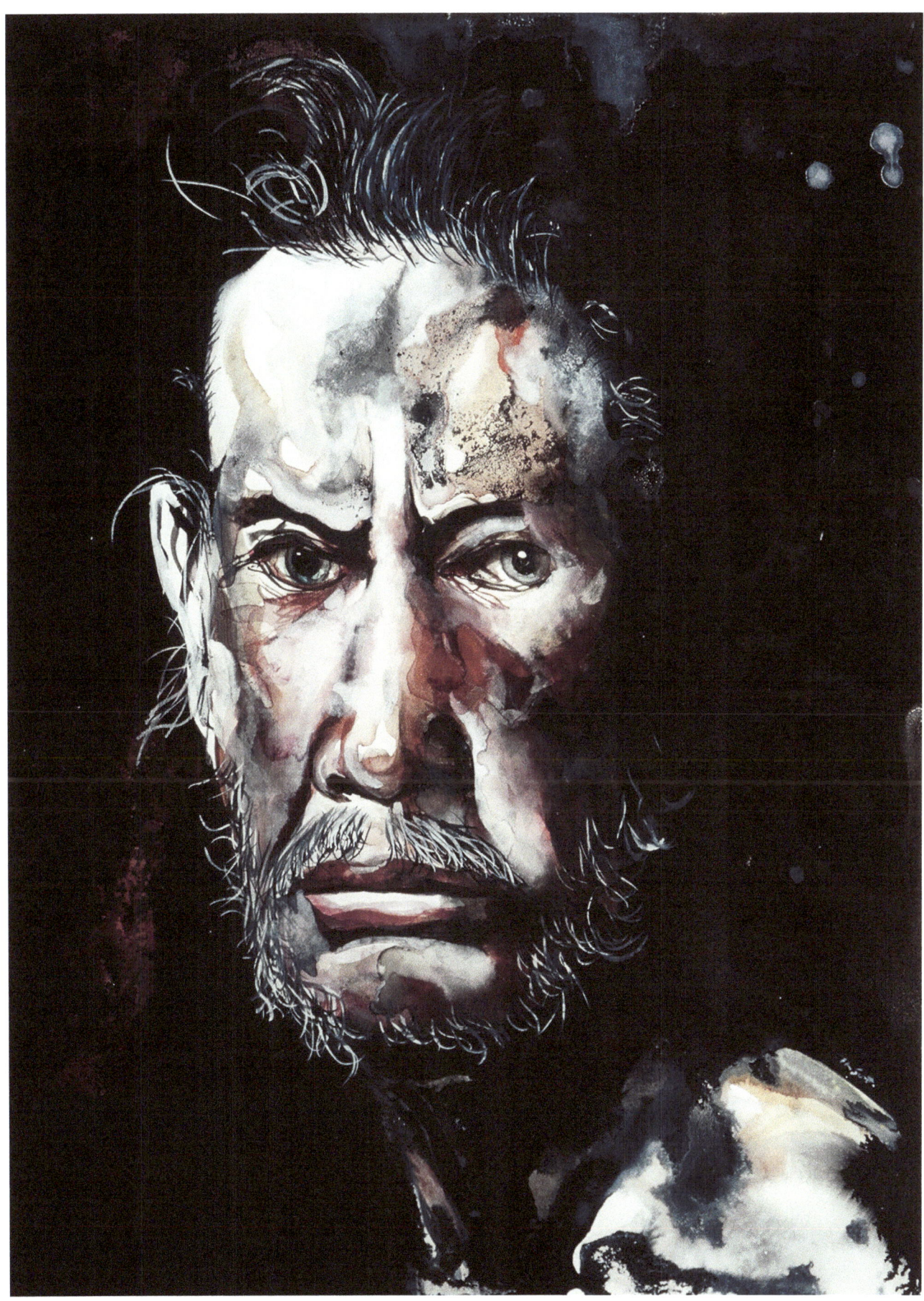

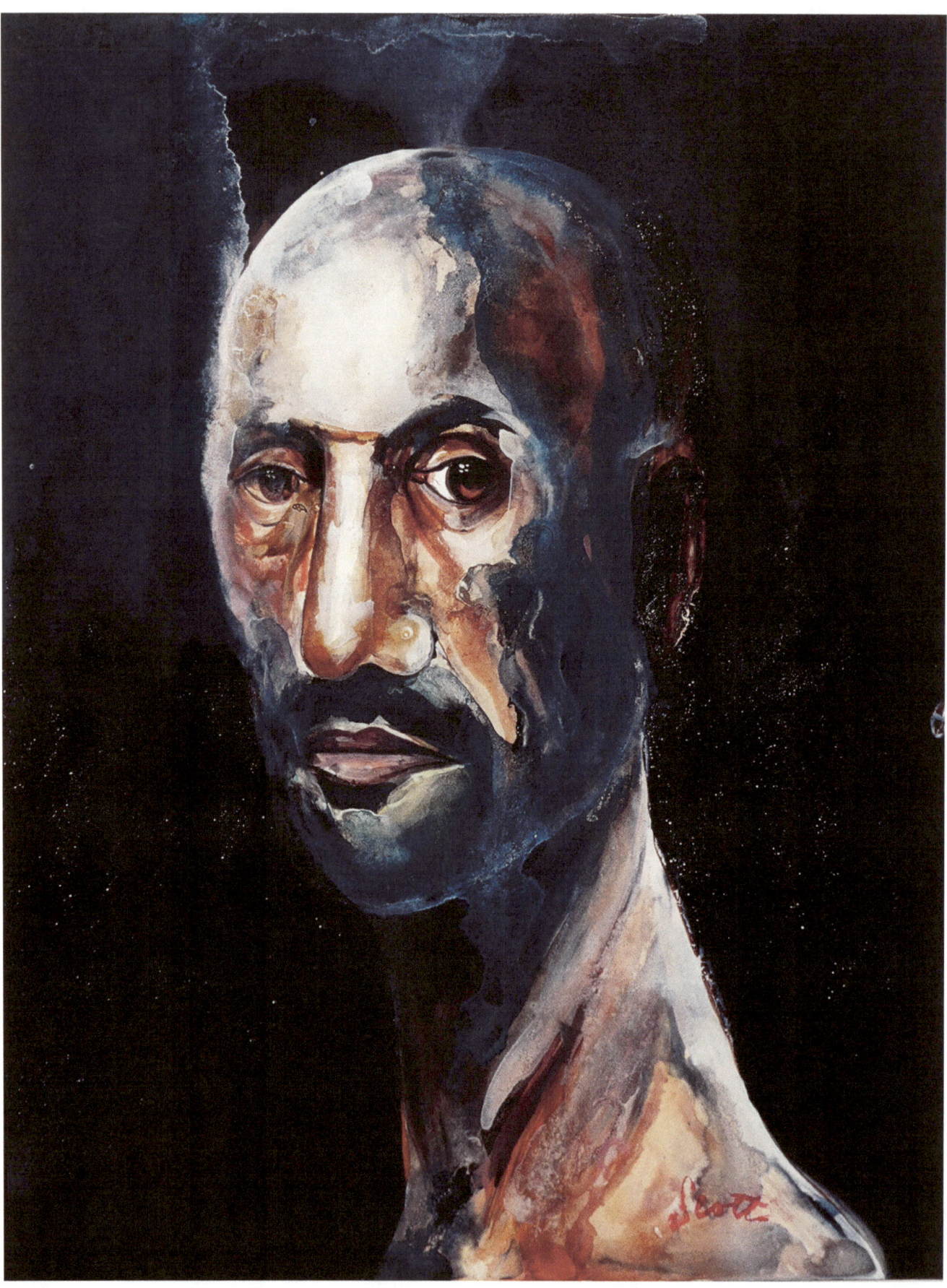

The Kurd

ink, watercolours and gouache on paper

12" x 9"

Aesthete Boxer

ink, watercolours and gouache on paper

12" x 9"

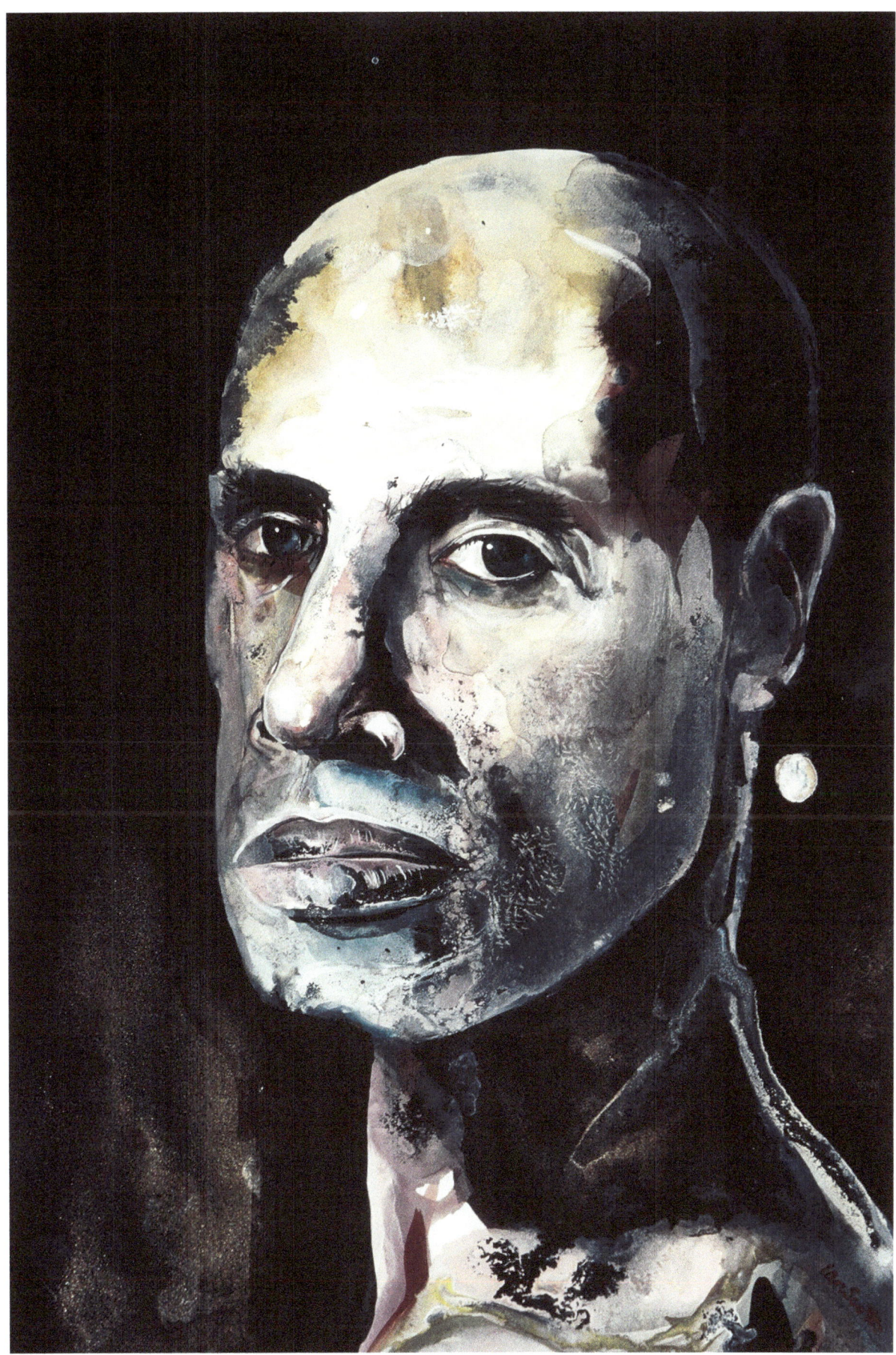

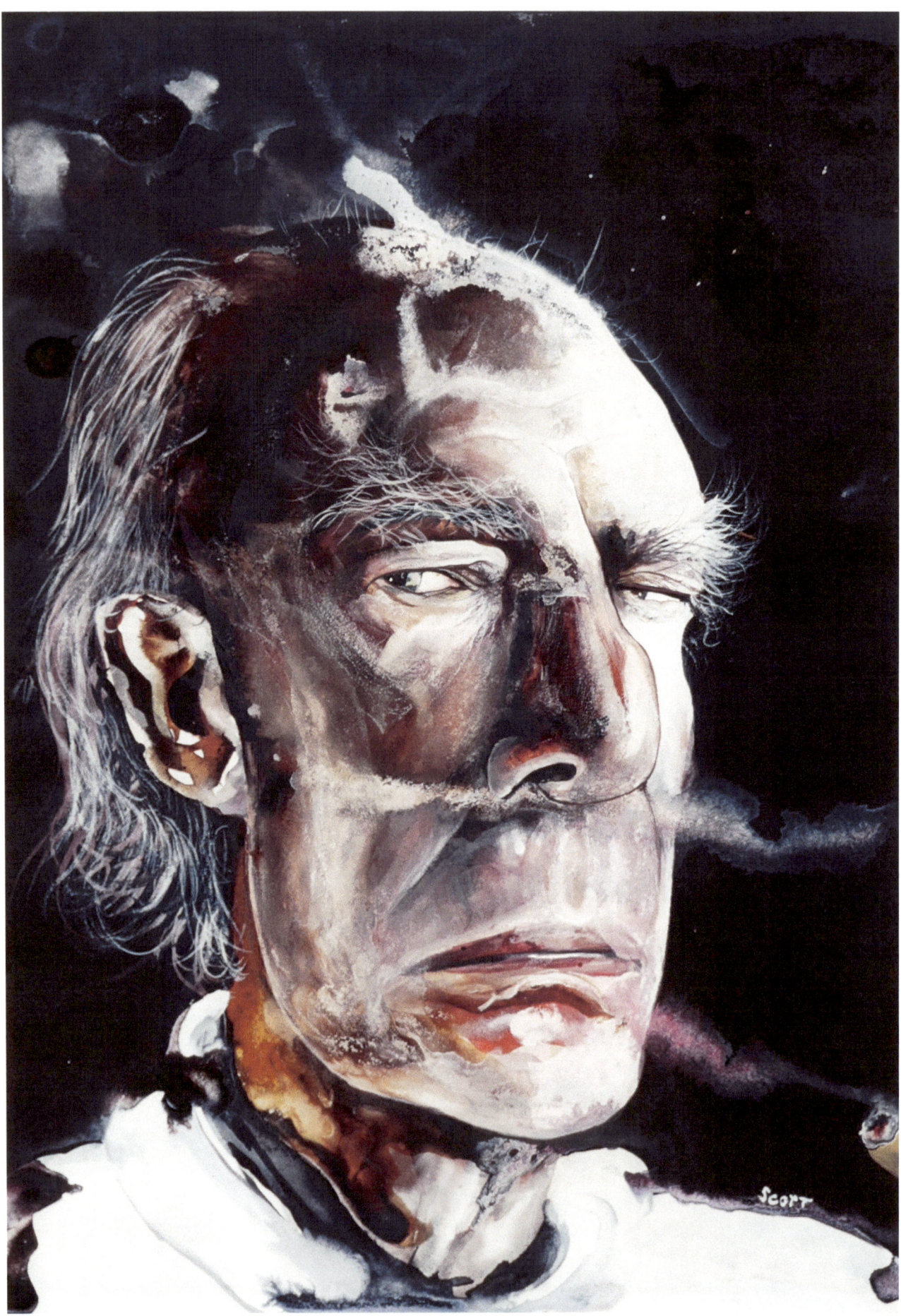

The Doctor

ink, watercolours and gouache on paper

12" x 9"

Pierre

ink, watercolours and gouache on paper

12" x 9"

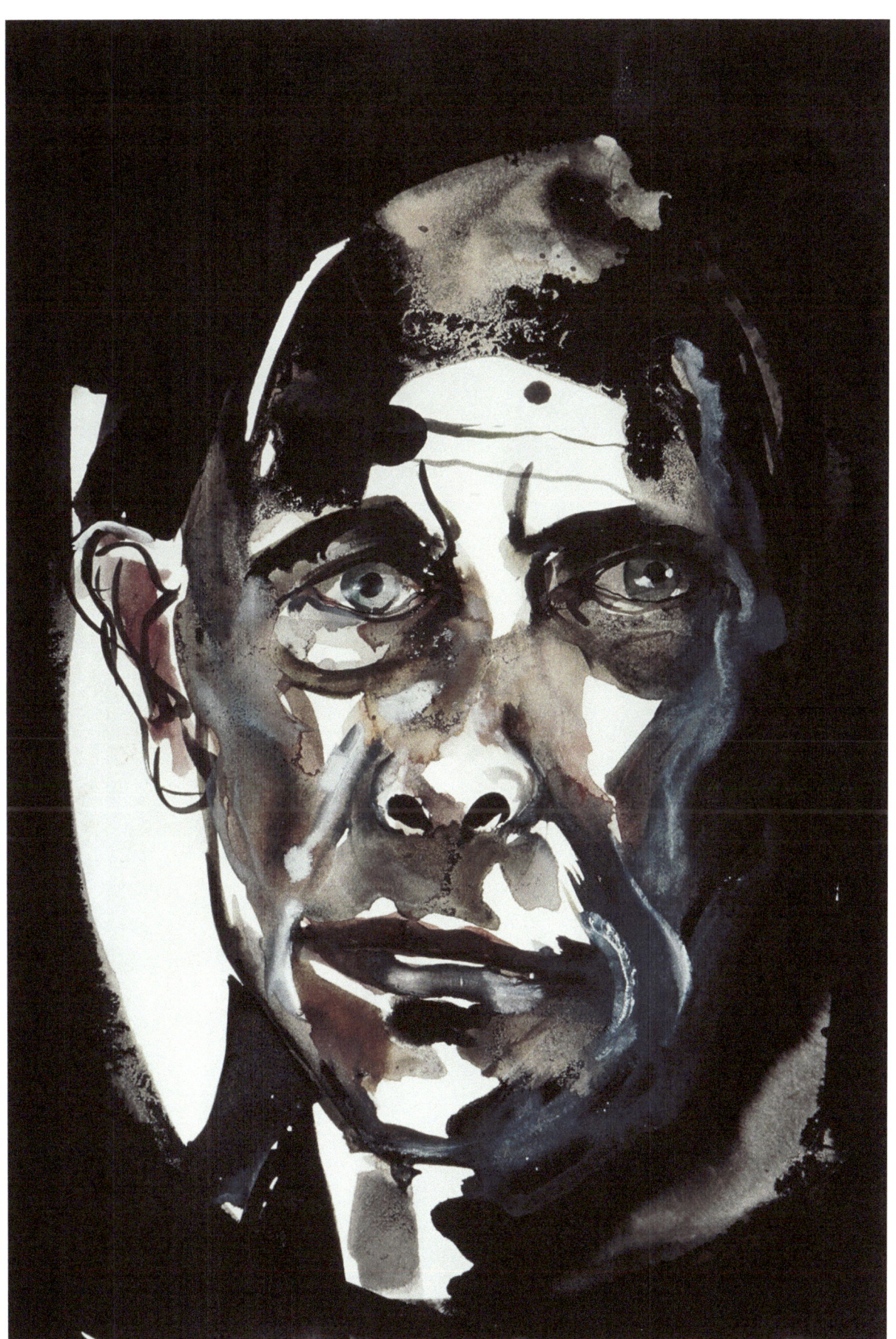

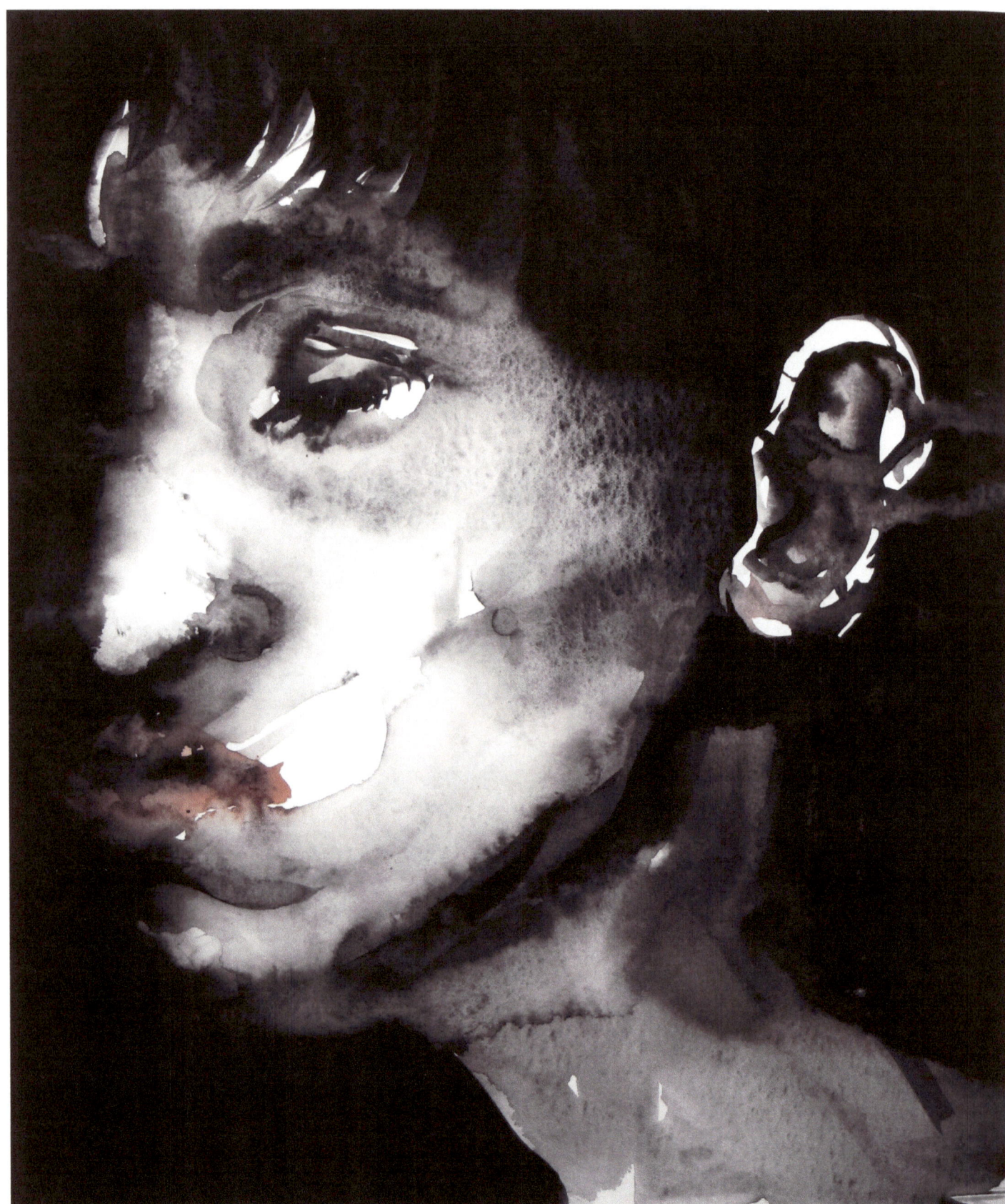

Autistic Profile

ink, watercolours and gouache on paper

12" x 9"

Hans der Aesthete

ink, watercolours and gouache on paper

12" x 9"

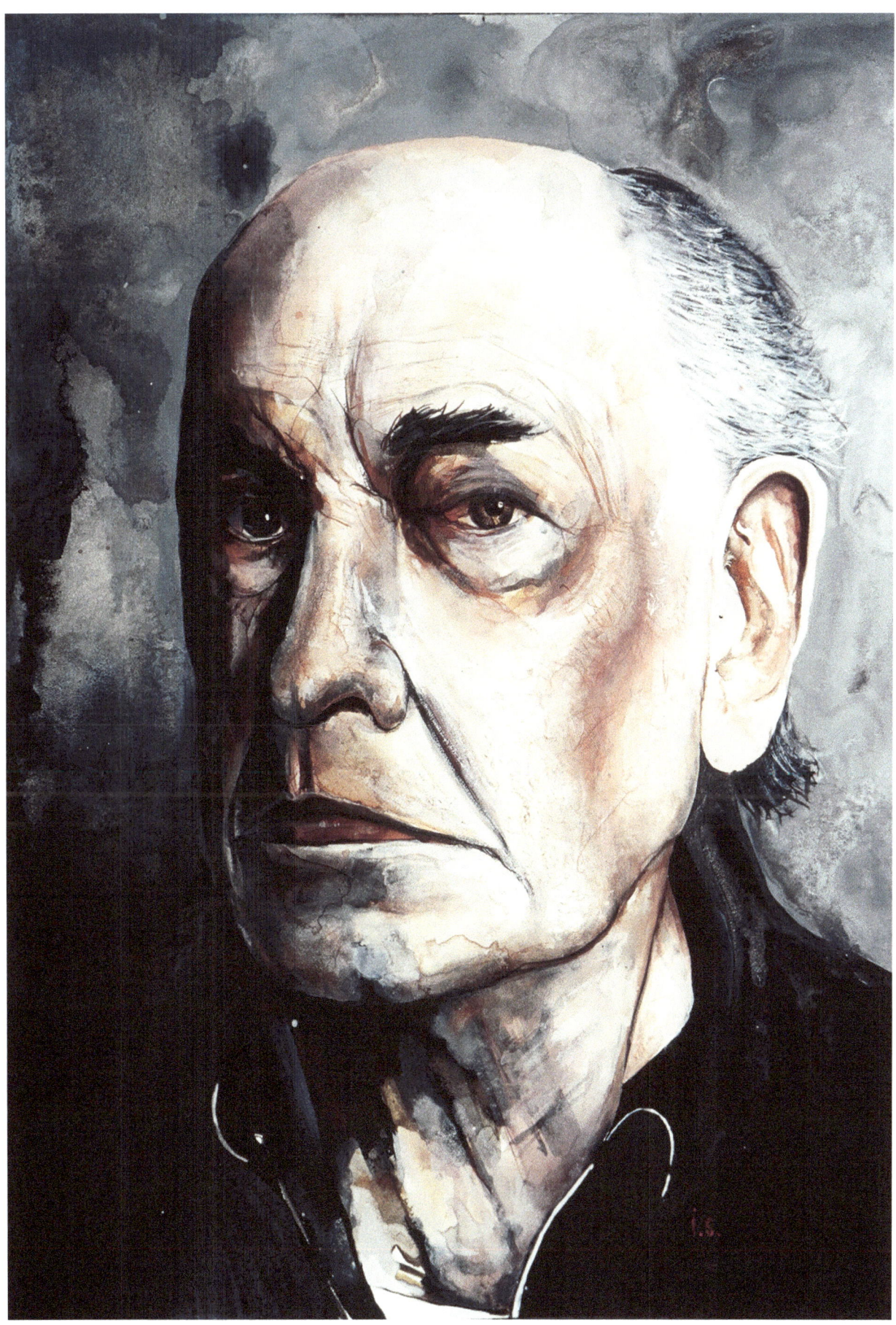

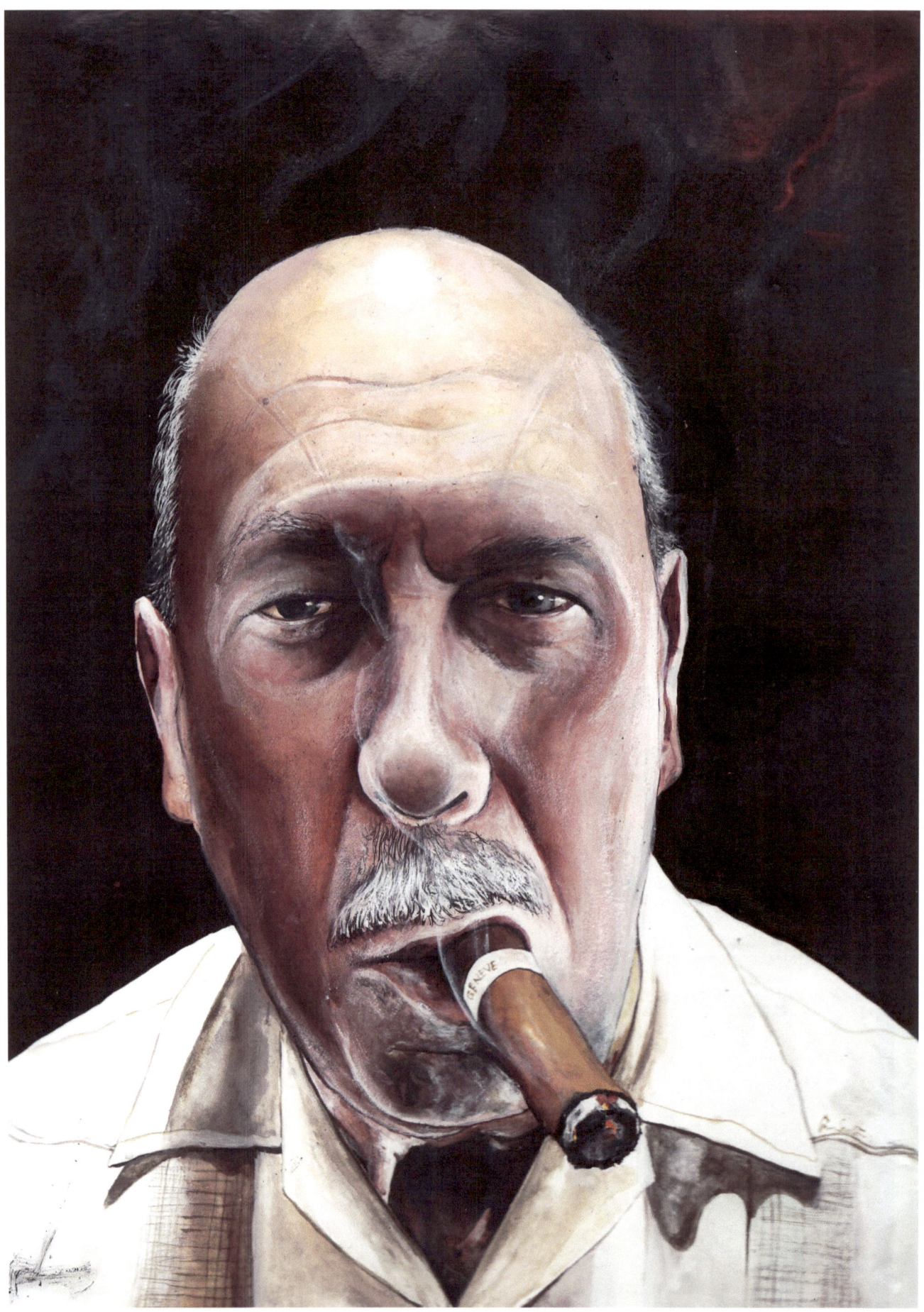

Cuban George 57th St Shop

ink, watercolours and gouache on paper

12" x 9"

Ukrainian Boxer

ink, watercolours and gouache on paper

12" x 9"

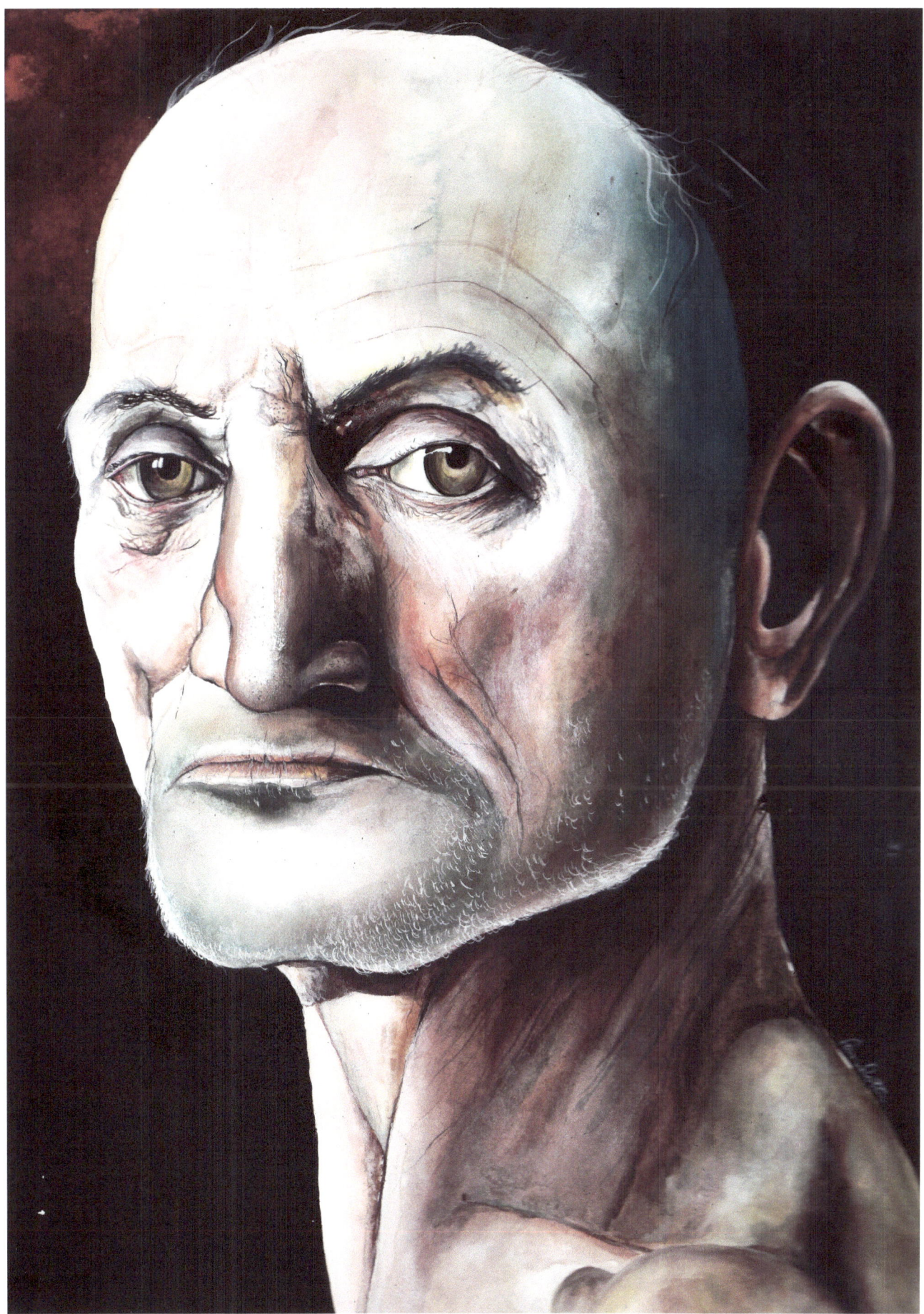

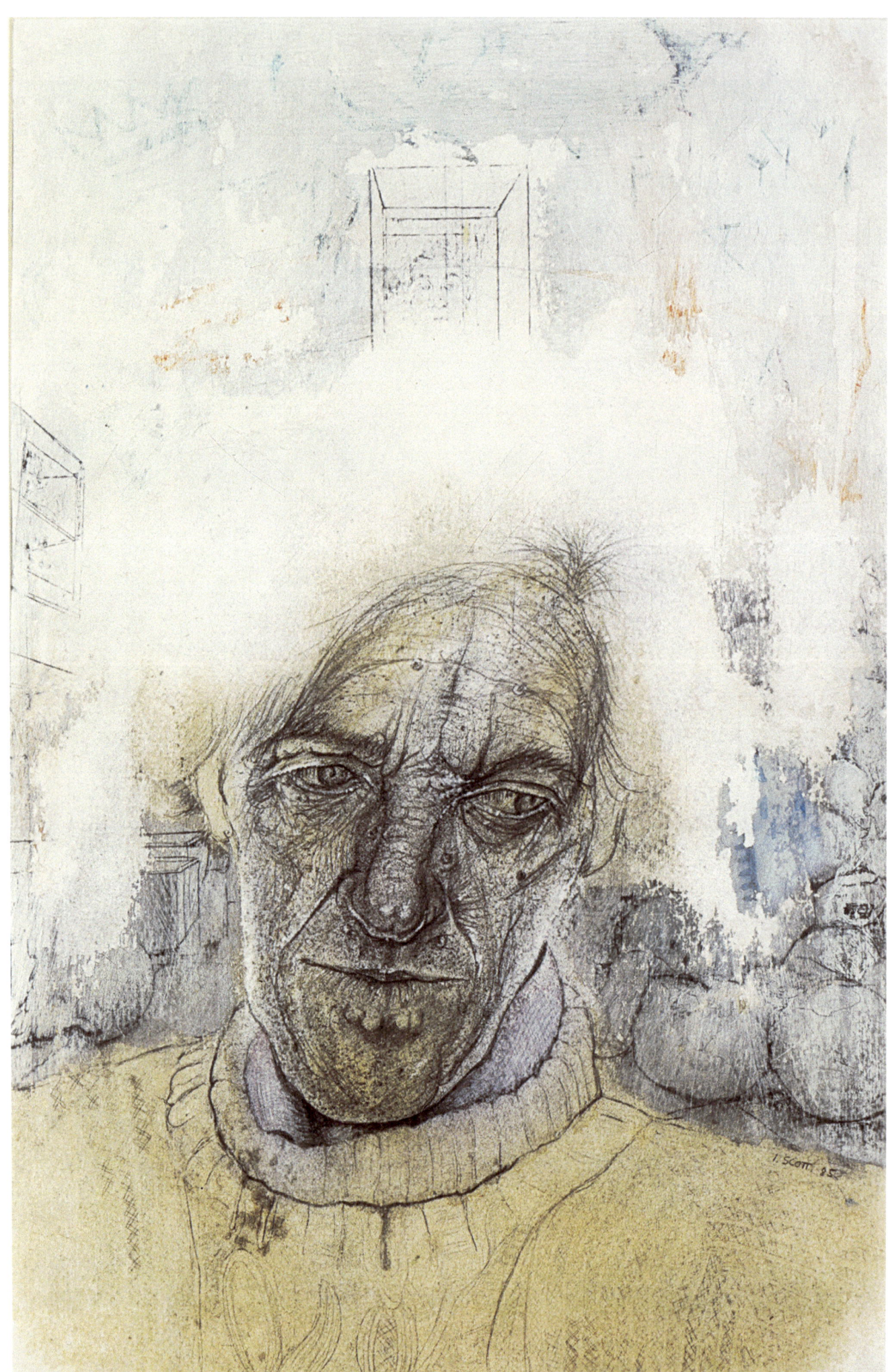

George Mackay Brown Portraits 1985-95

George Mackay Brown was regarded by many as the finest Scottish poet of the 20th century and was certainly the best known. He was short- listed for the Man Booker prize in 1994 and lived almost his entire life in the Orkney Islands in the extreme north of Scotland.

He converted to Catholicism in his late 30s and Catholic mysticism continued to be a strong theme in his work until end of his life.

"I had been introduced to his work in High School. He lived near Wick.

In 1985 after my graduation, I wrote to him. I was using bits of his poems as titles for a series of etchings I was doing, so I contacted him and asked if I could draw him.

Well, he wrote back to me and said - 'I don't see why you would want to make a portrait of me but if you want to that would be alright', and that I could come visit him.

I stayed in a youth hostel nearby, found where he lived and rang the bell. George came to the door in the cable-knit fisherman's jumper he always wore. He had big blue eyes like orbs and hair spinning out like effluvia.

He was a little uncomfortable a first, but we started to get on quite well and had four days there. You could tell when he liked you; he put whiskey in the tea. The whiskey spilled onto the bottom of the drawing and I used it to start the color.

I went out there with a girl from California I had met at school. She kept him busily talking away while I drew as we listened to the wind blowing down the chimney as an undersong.

On the last day, Mary Pat got all these books of George's and we took them to him and he signed them all for us.

Our friendship stayed until he died in 1996. He wrote letters to me every week through the whole time.'"

- Ian Scott

In the Sun's Last House,

pencil, gesso watercolour, whiskey and tea on paper

18" x 14"

Collection of Aberdeen Art gallery

"From his poem- Maeshowe, which is an ancient chambered cairn-an earthwork with a long tunnel in its center, designed to create complete silence. On the summer solstice, the position of the sun as it rises goes along the tunnel and lights up symbols on back of the wall. I tried to recreate the atmosphere here."   *- Ian Scott*

All images 1985-1995

Following pages: George Mackay Brown, 12" x 9" pencil, I and II

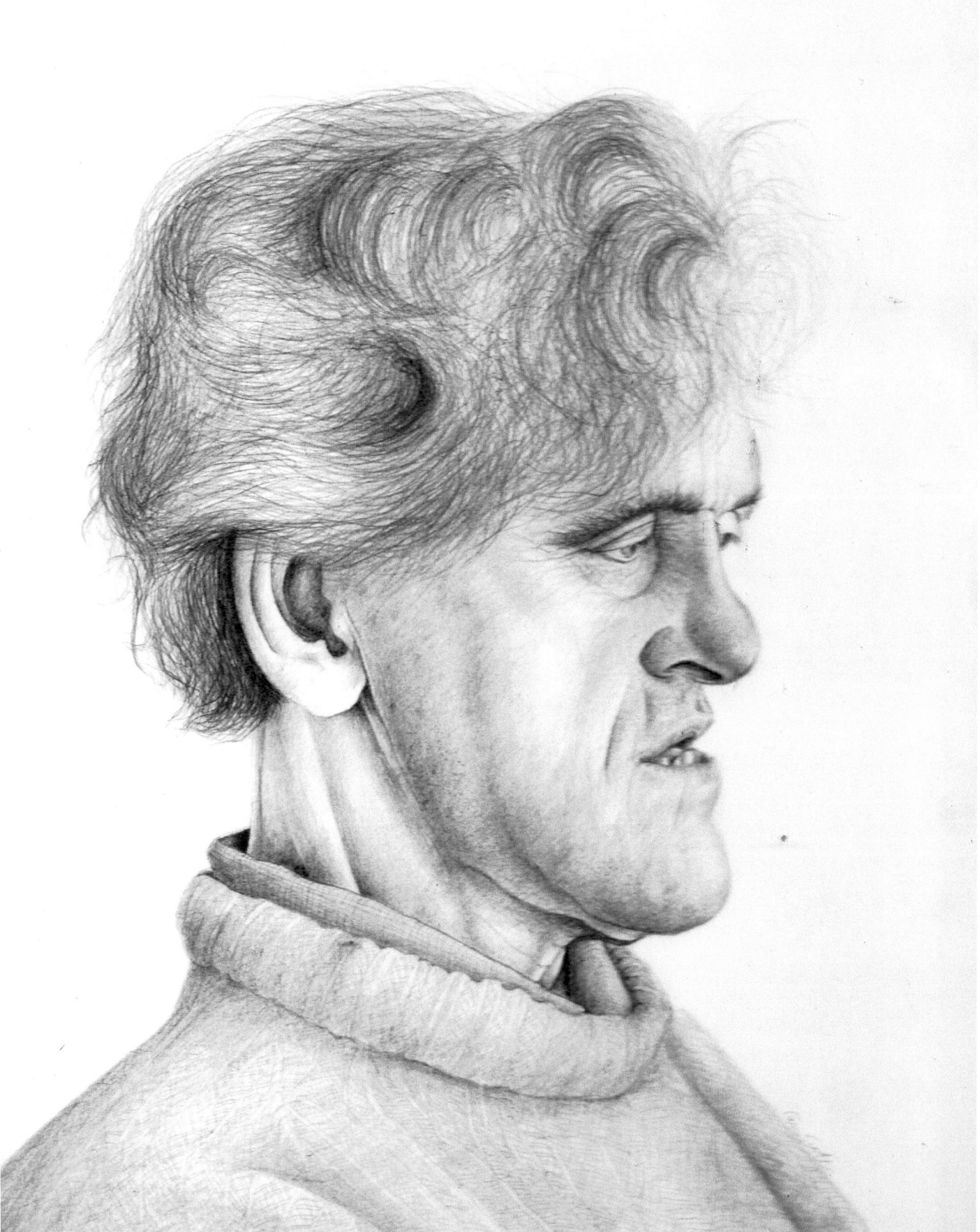

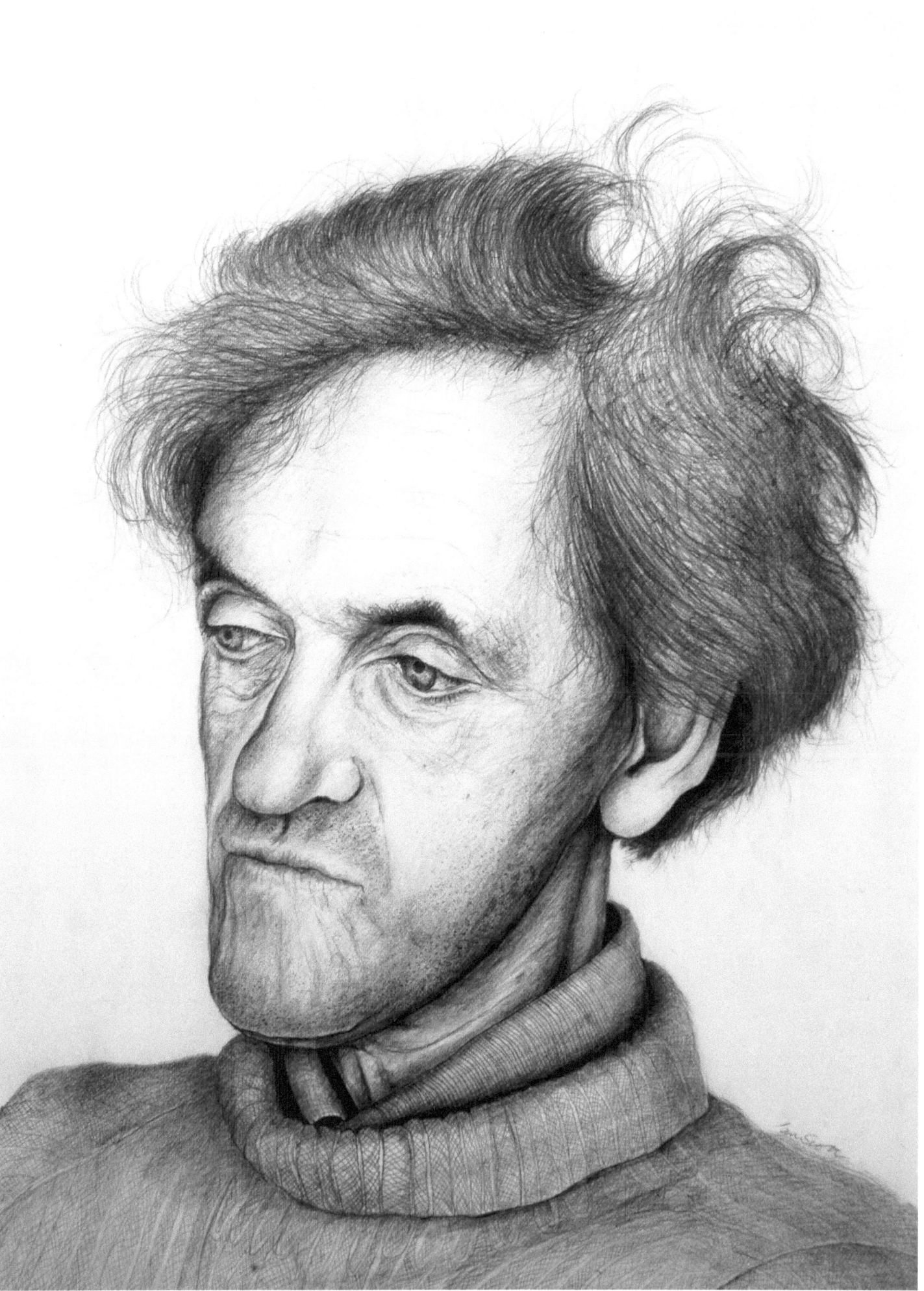

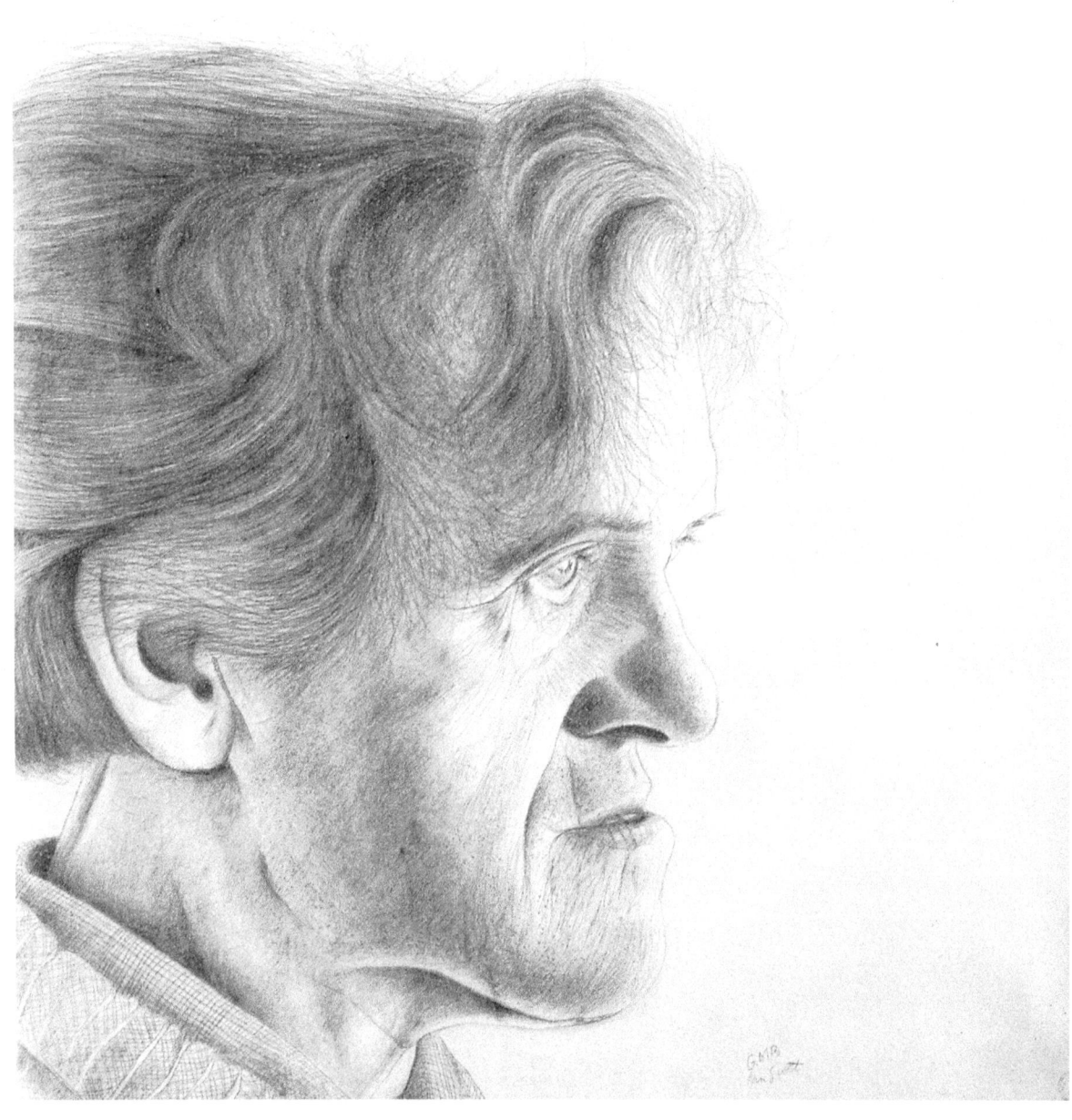

Above: George Mackay Brown, silverpoint on prepared paper, 10" x 8"

Opposite: George Mackay Brown, silverpoint on prepared paper, 11" x 8"   Collection of Scottish National Portrait Gallery

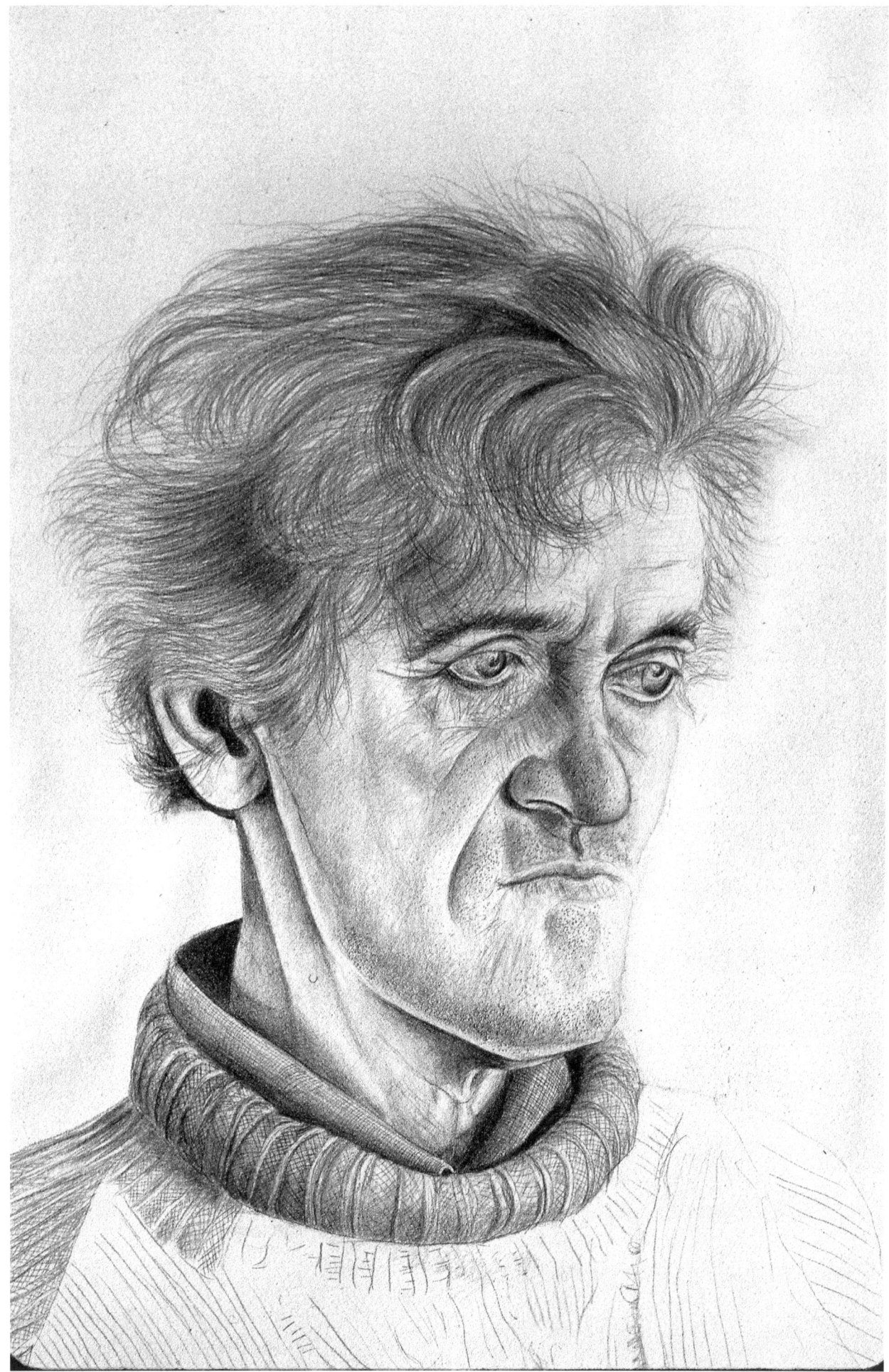

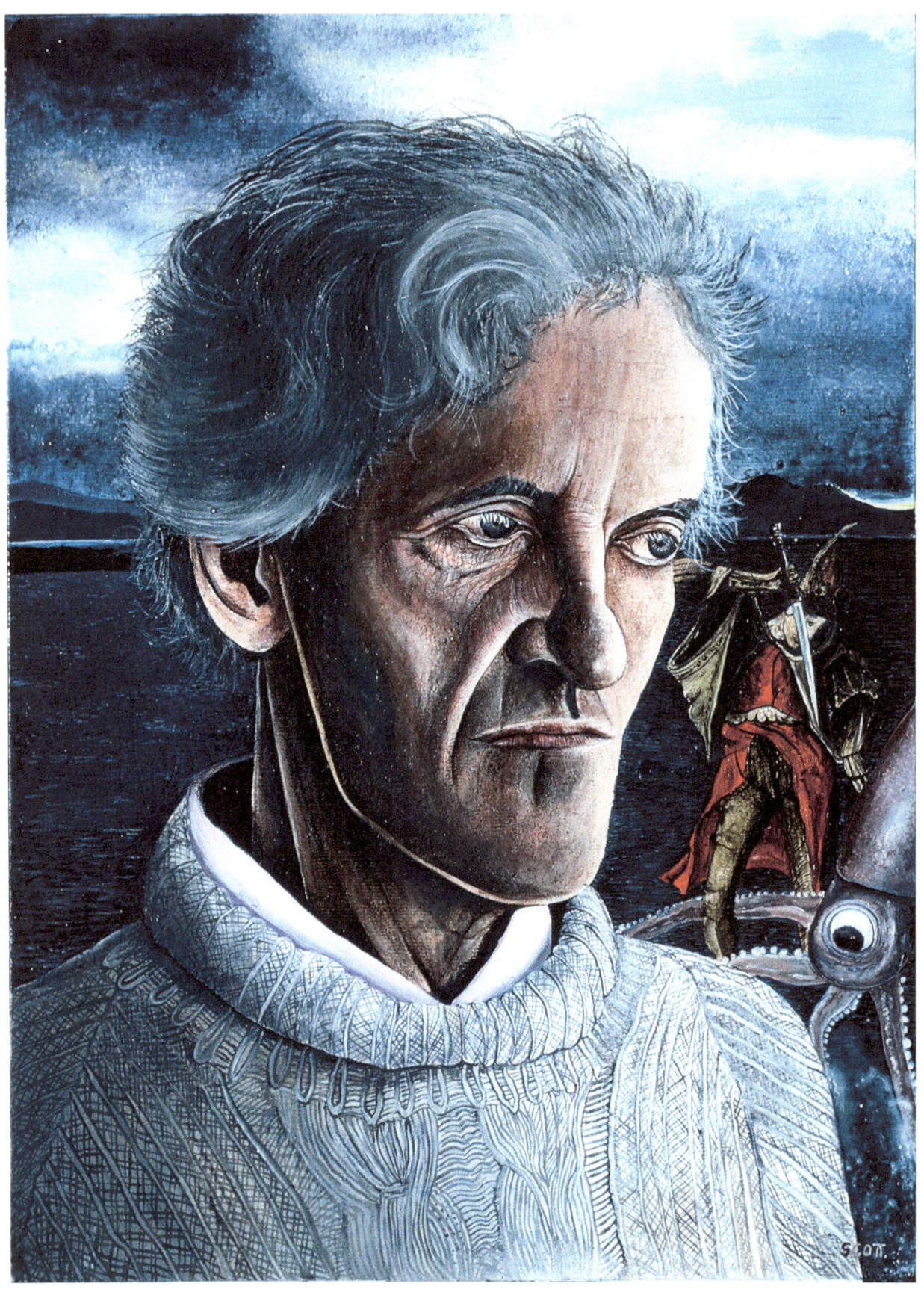

Above: George Mackay Brown with St Magnus and squid oil on paper, 12" x 9"

Opposite: Large life study of George Mackay Brown, oil on paper, 36" x 24"

Collection of Stromness Museum , Orkney

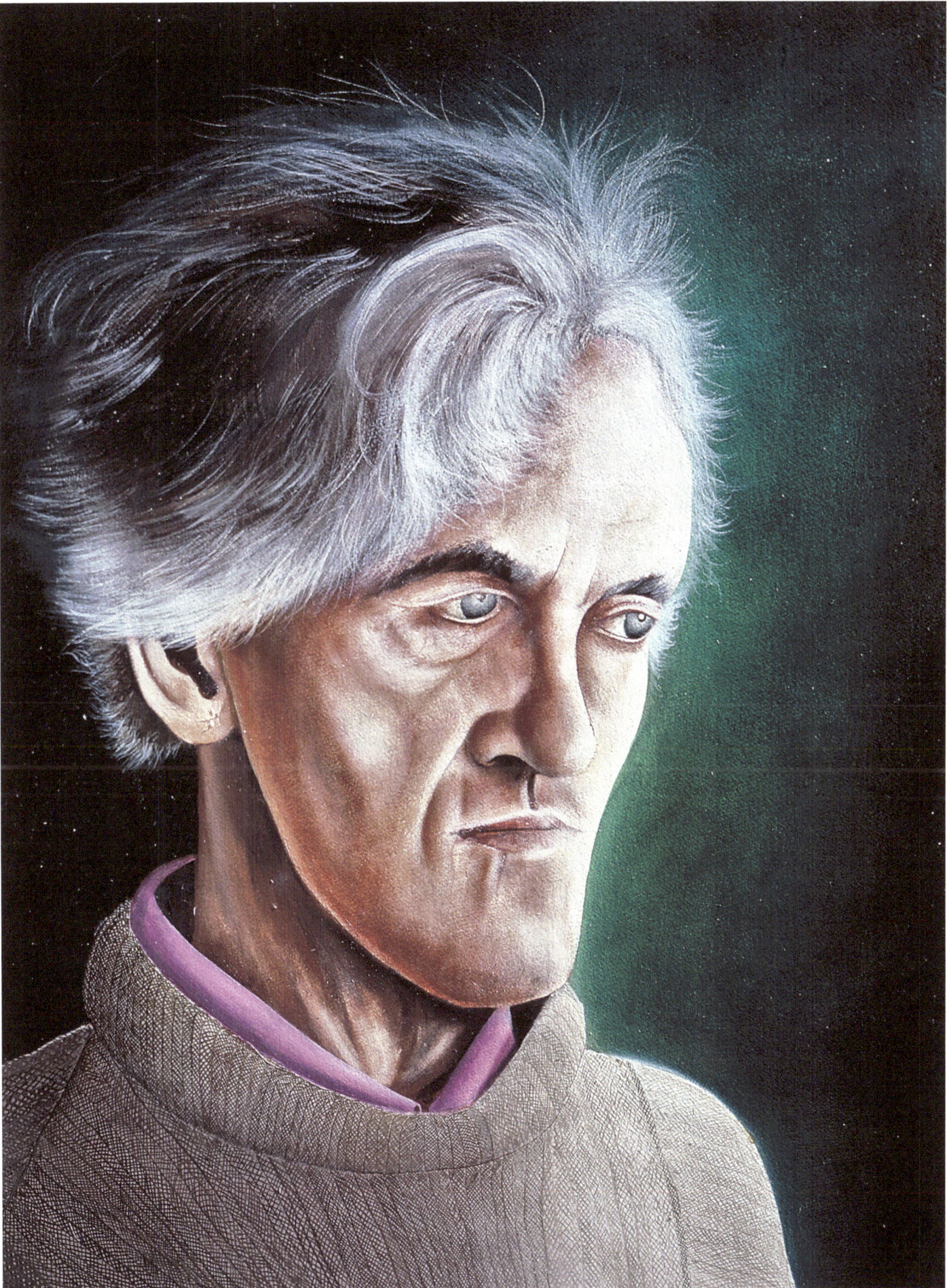

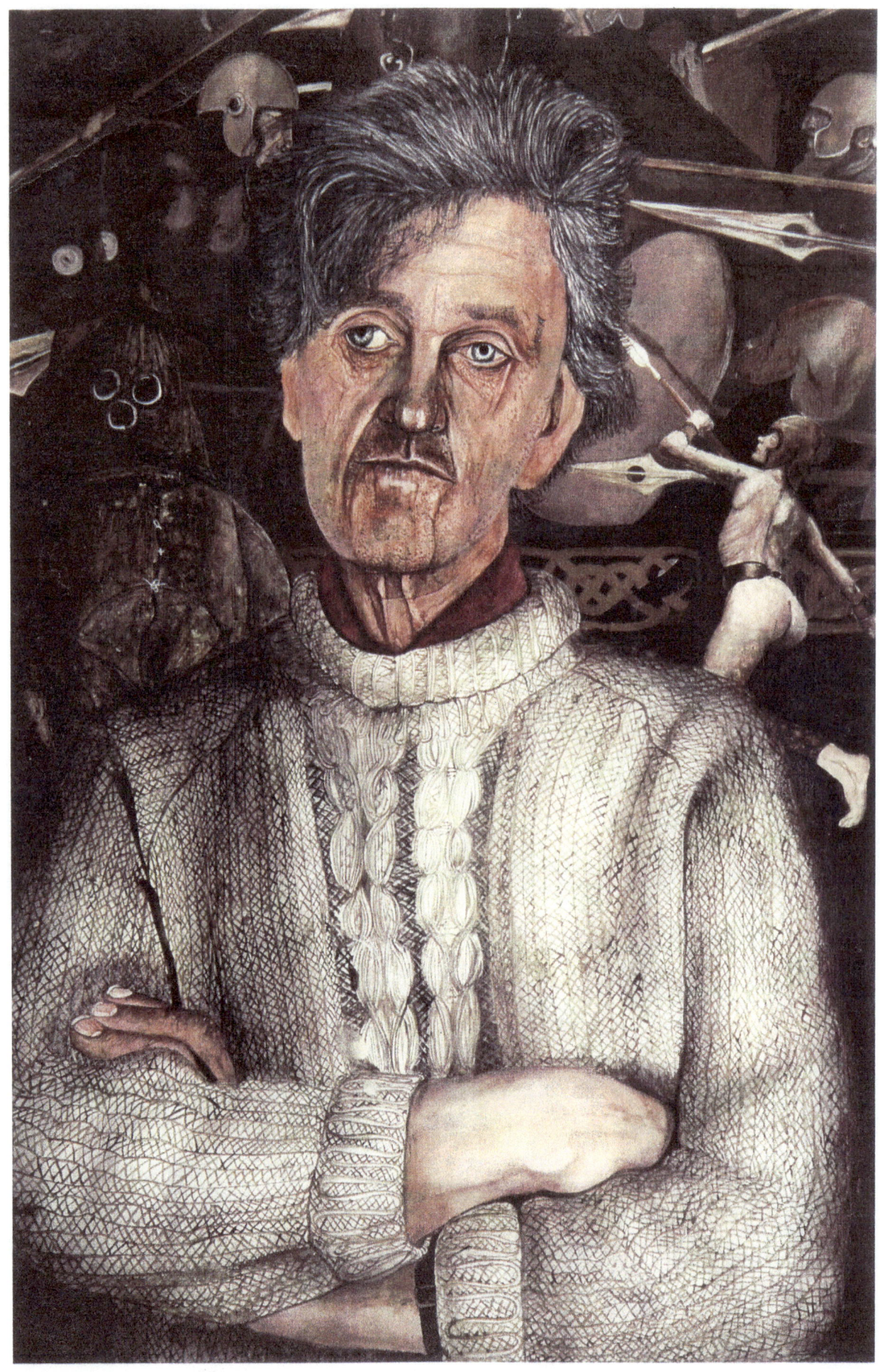

George Mackay Brown Holding Court, watercolour on paper, 24" x 18"

G M Brown
3 Mayburn Court
STROMNESS
Orkney
KW16 3DH

30 Jan 1986

Dear Ian

Many thanks for your letter.
I am glad you're working
consistently and happily :
also to hear a discriminating
person here and there has
the good sense to purchase a
work.

I am glad we're drawing
to a close of January : it has
been a harsh month ... I
took Hogmanay & New Year
very easily — I grow to
dislike that time of year.
30 years ago I revelled in it.

I am busy working on
some stories. One was full of
difficulties & problems, like a
labyrinth where I had to
find a way back out of
dead ends and cul-de-sacs.
Now I think I see a way
through. But I may be wrong.

The sun is shining today
and it is very cold, and I
have Nora's black cat Gypsy
sleeping near me and 2
workmen outside are chipping
the iron railing of Mayburn
preparatory to painting it.
It's like a clanging & wild

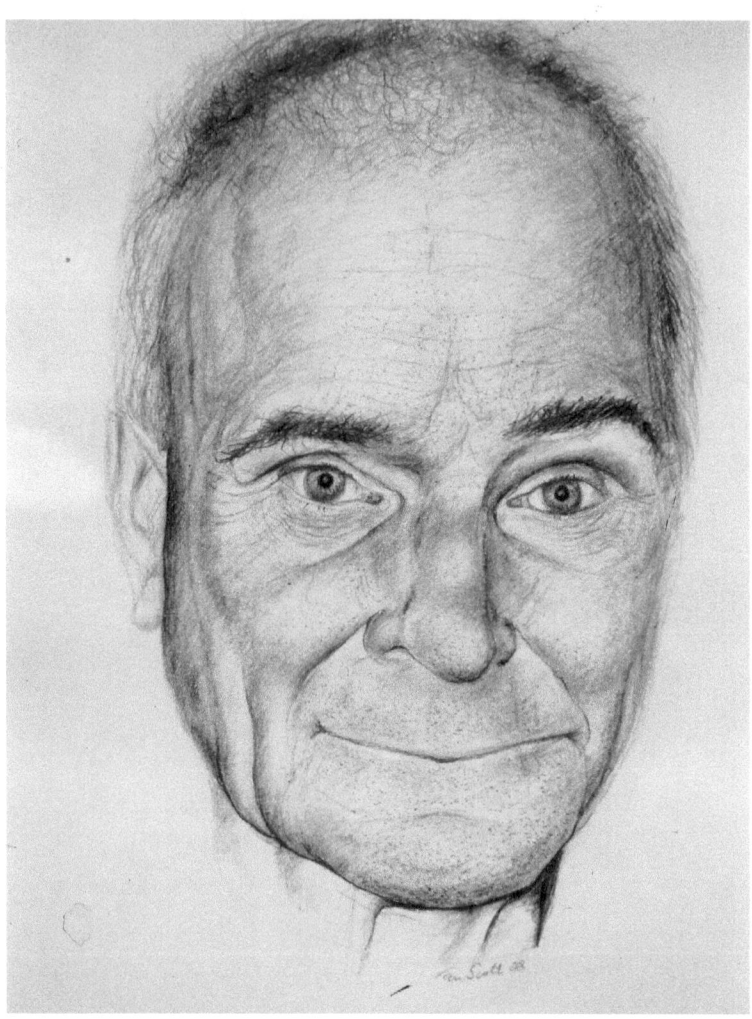

"My first introduction to the work of Sir Peter Maxwell Davies was in the late 1970s. I was attending a mime class in Covent Garden, London led by the master Lindsey Kemp.

I mentioned to a woman I met there that I was making a medieval film called Mandrake. She turned out to be a BBC record archivist and she suggested PMD's Tenebrae super Gesualdo for the soundtrack.

I was very impressed with the music and over the next few years attended several concerts when he was conducting the Scottish Symphony Orchestra and did drawings of him. It had also transpired that he had moved to Orkney from England to obtain silence for his composing and made best friends with George Mackay Brown. The two of them then began collaborating. Sir Peter Maxwell Davies set up the St. Magnus festival in Orkney, which became one of the world's principle classical music festivals.

Sir Peter Maxwell Davies and I are in regular correspondence and have been brought together by our mutual love of the work of George Mackay Brown and Orkney of course."

- Ian Scott

Above: Sir Peter Maxwell Davies, Pencil Study, 12" x 9" 2008

Opposite: Sir Peter Maxwell Davies, oils on panel, 24" X 18", 2009

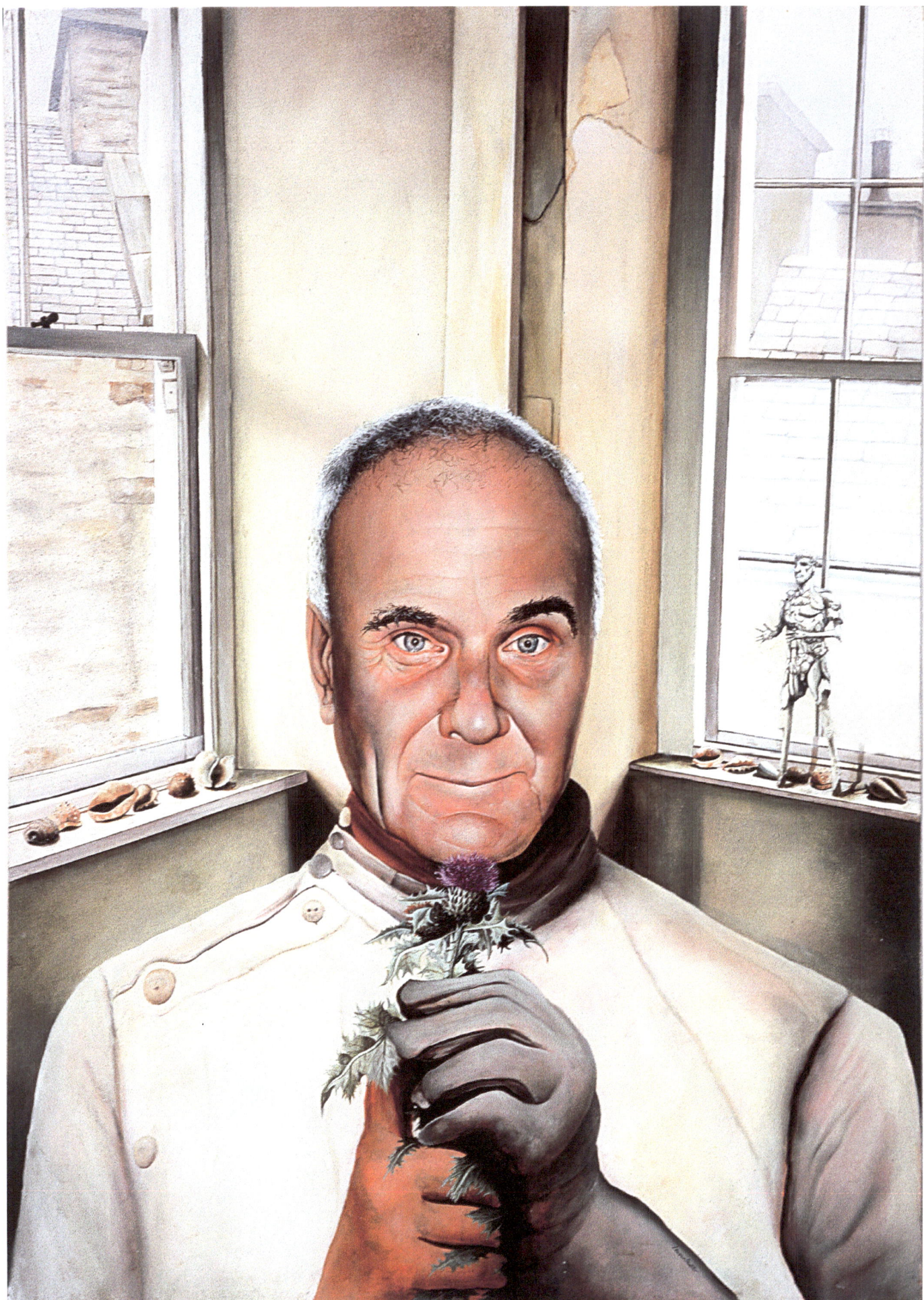

The Reverend RR Sinclair of Wick,

the oldest Wee Free Minister in Scotland.

"He was a First World War veteran and was shot in the rear in1917.

The bullet popped out ten years later and he kept it on the shelf beside his collection of historic bibles.

RR preached right up until death in his late 90s and was my next door neighbour."

- Ian Scott

RR Sinclair with Black and White Center of High Street, Wick, Caithness,

during his ministry.

oil on wood, 18" x 14", 2011

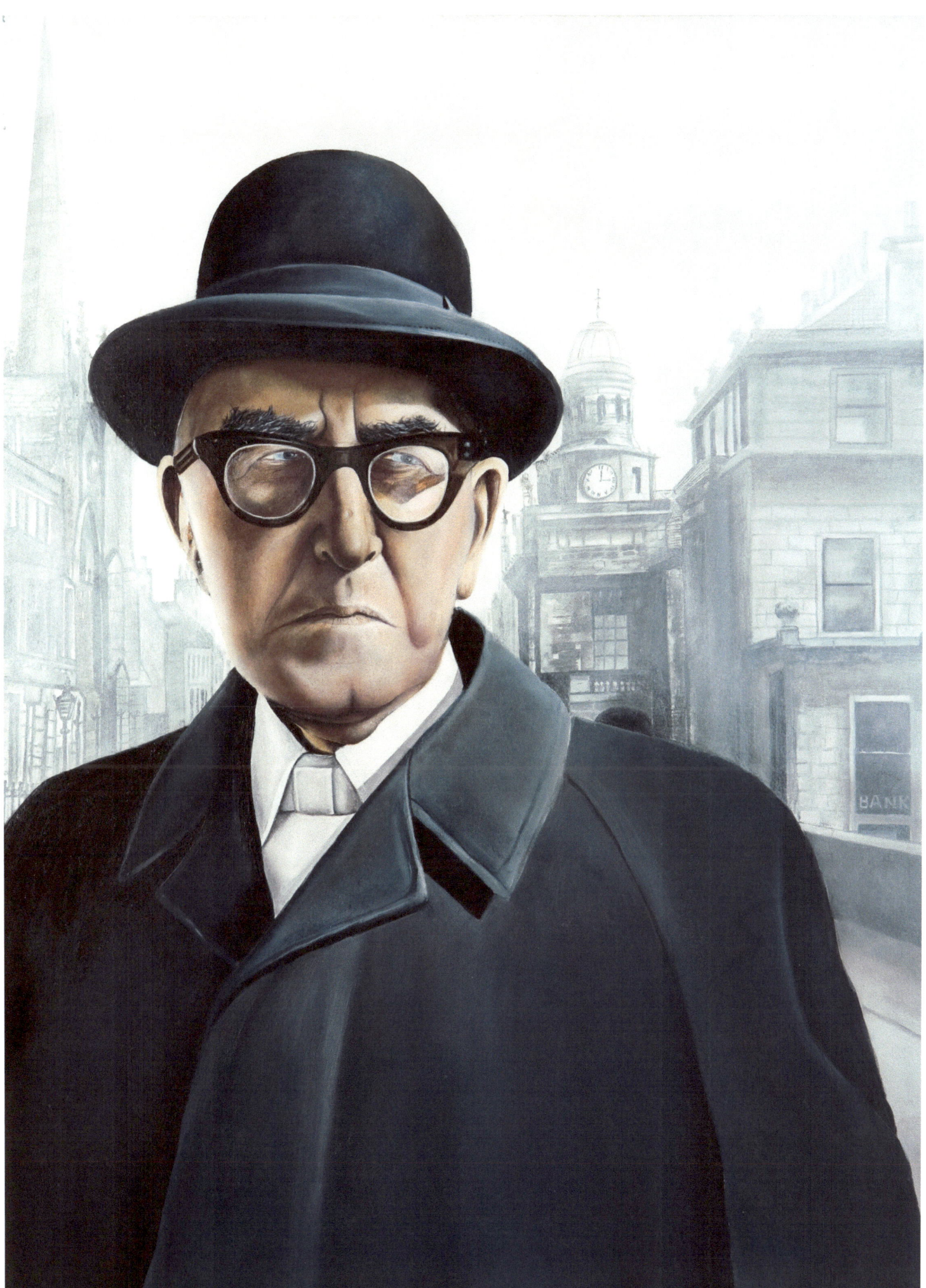

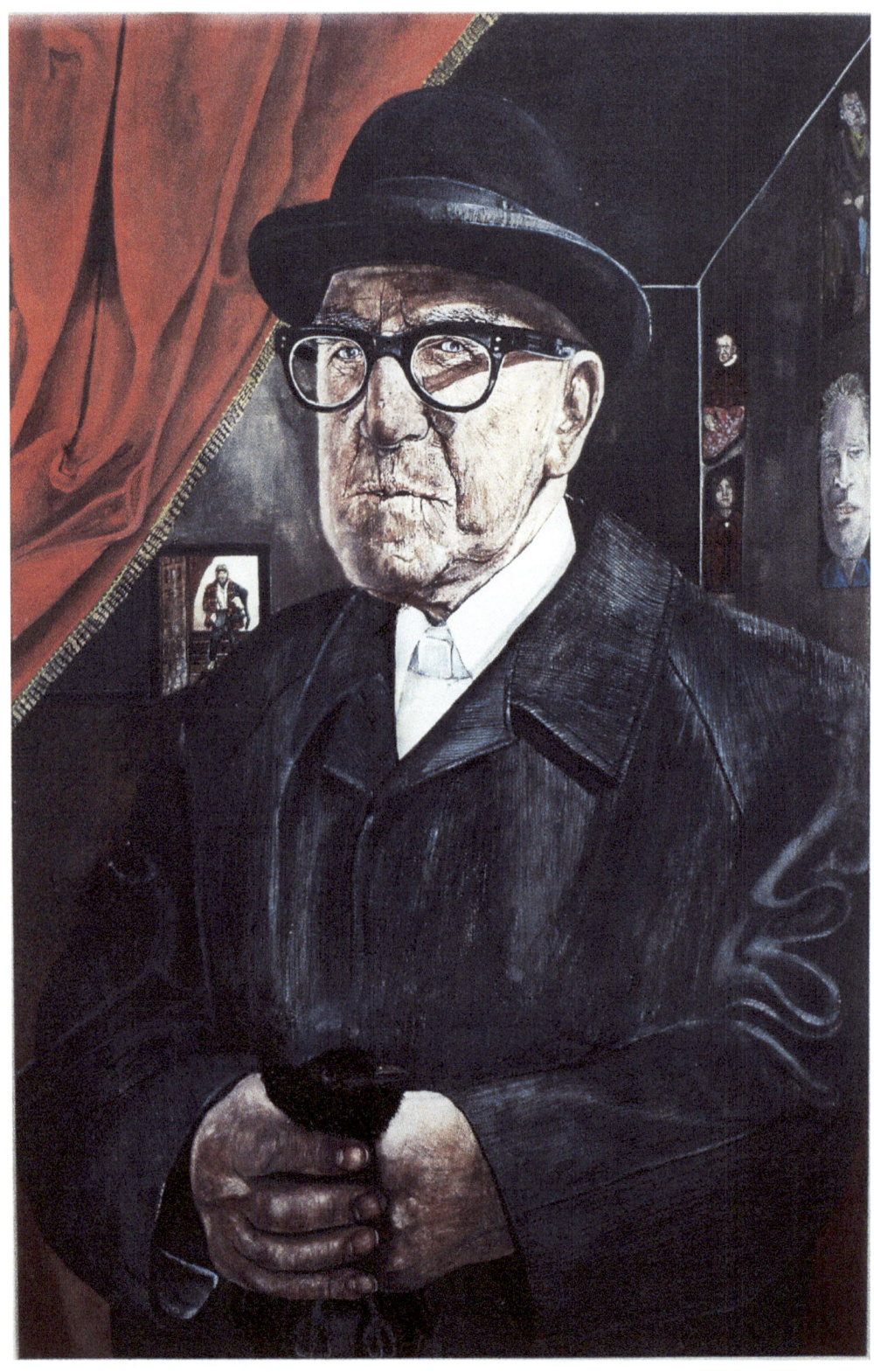

Above: Earlier watercolour study of the Rev RR Sinclair-

with imaginary background- 16" x 12" on paper

Opposite: Pencil study of the Reverend RR Sinclair, 16" x 12", 2011

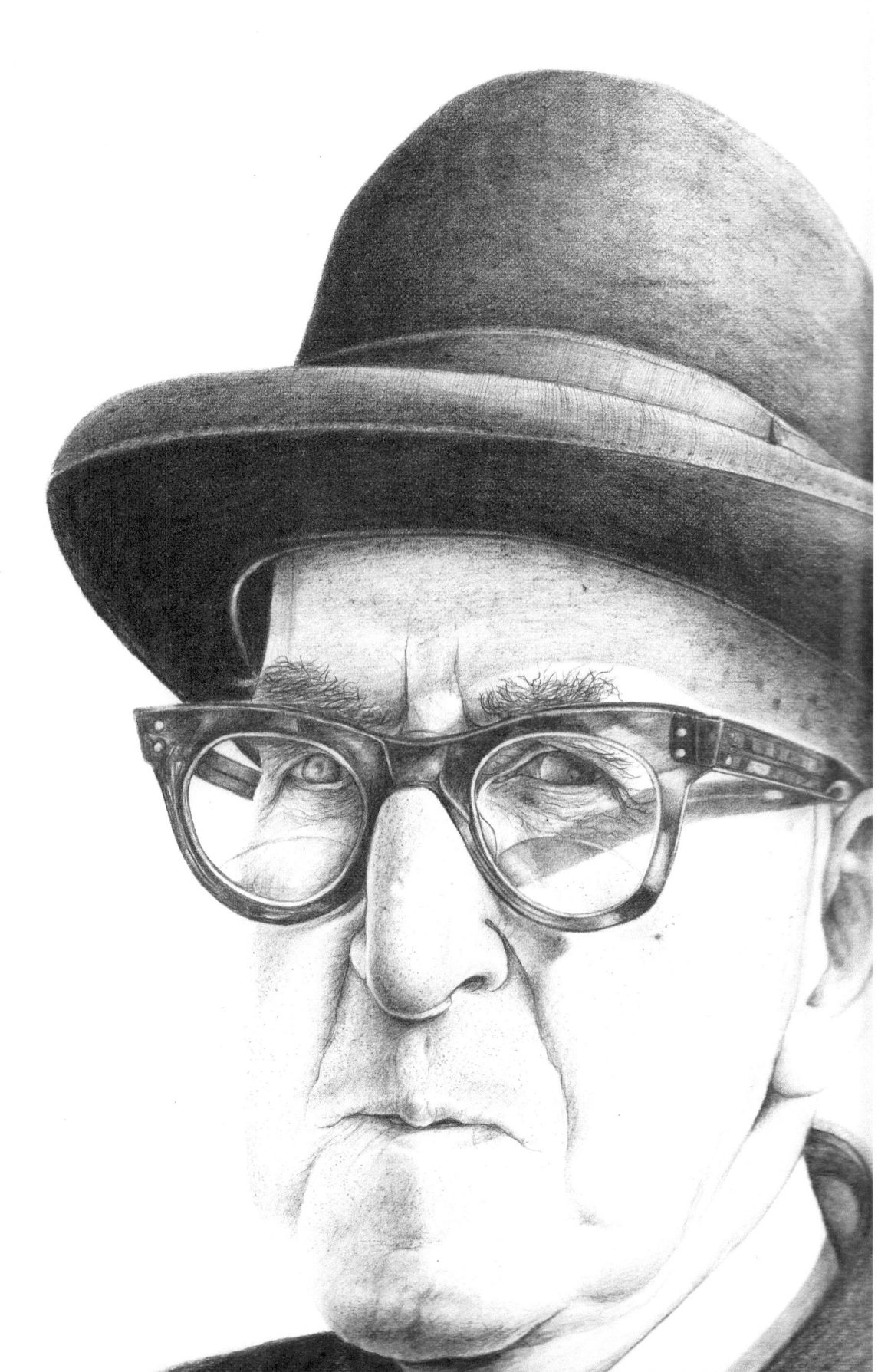

Portraits 2000-2011

Harbourmaster of Wick,
pencil, 12" x 9" 2011

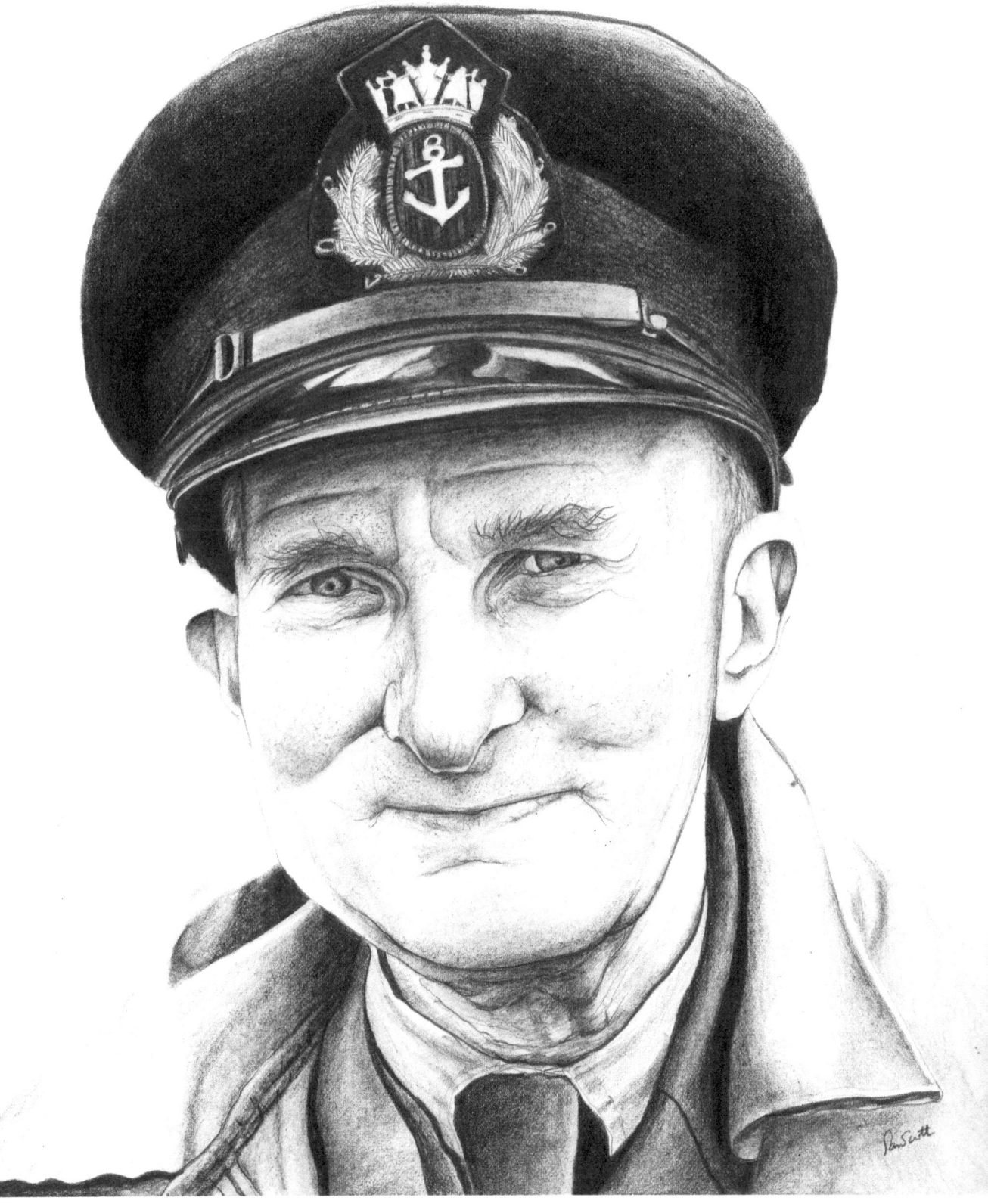

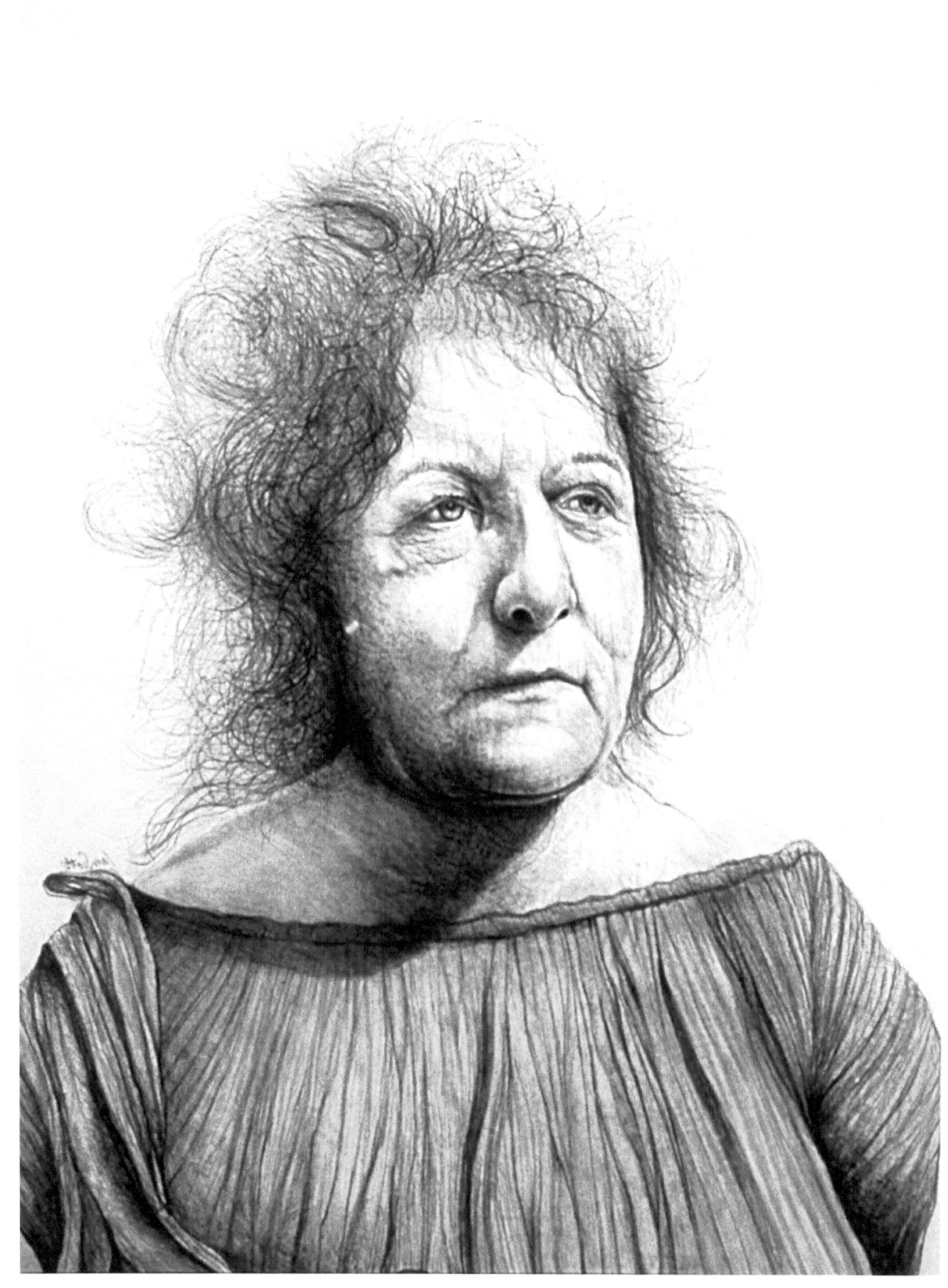

Medea pencil on paper, 18" x 14", 2005

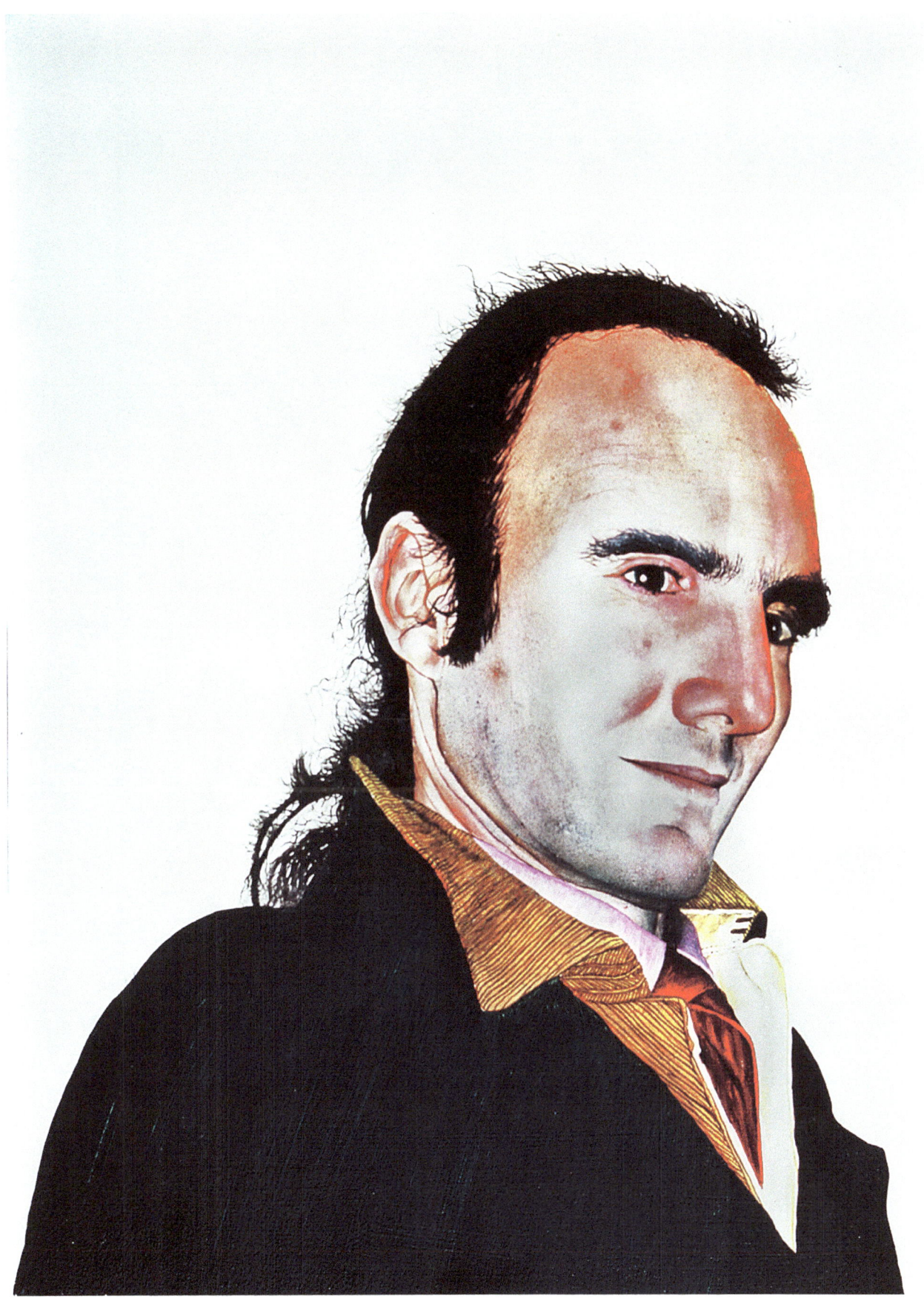

Steve, oil on panel, 16" x 12", 2003

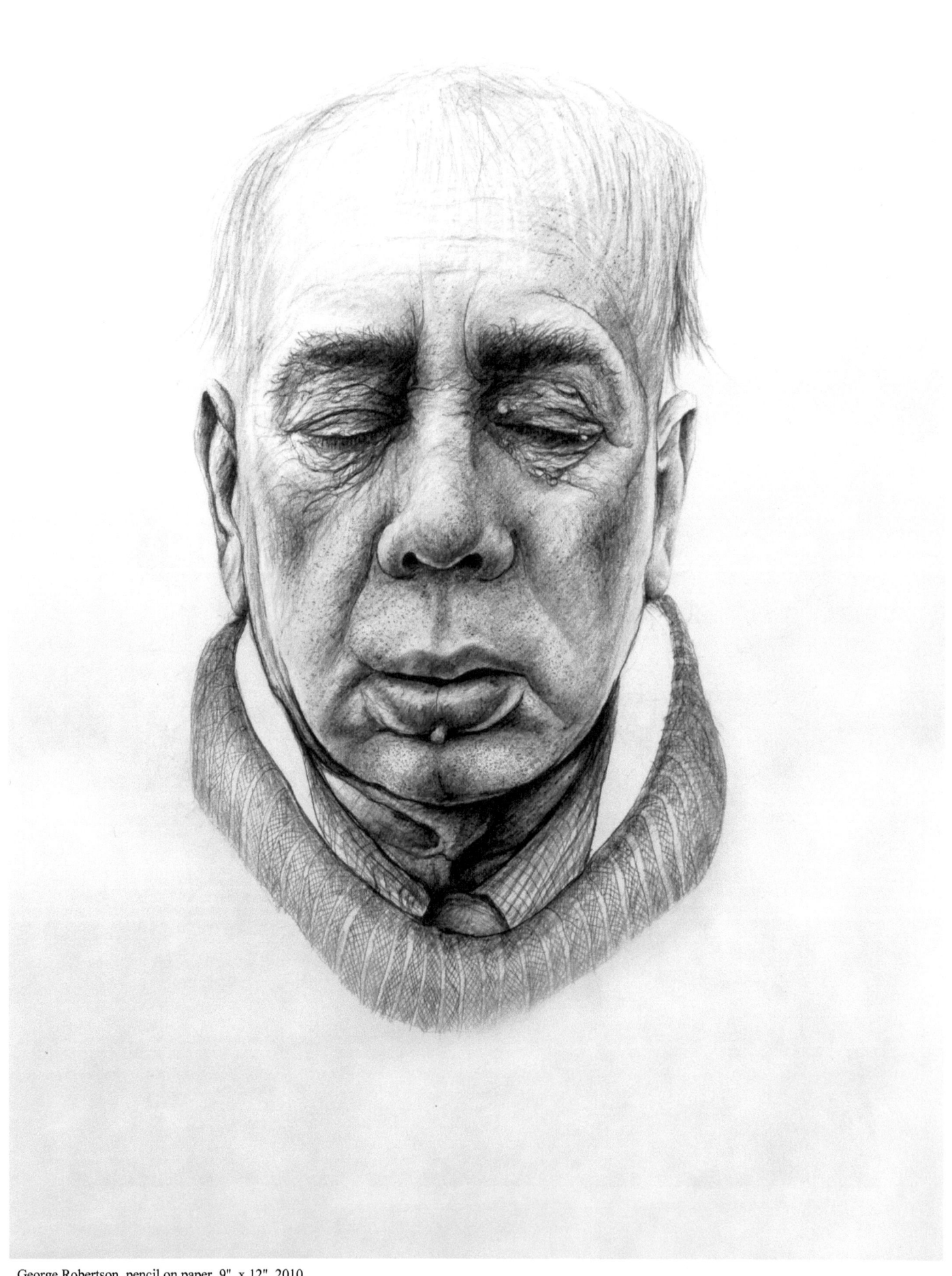

George Robertson, pencil on paper, 9" x 12", 2010

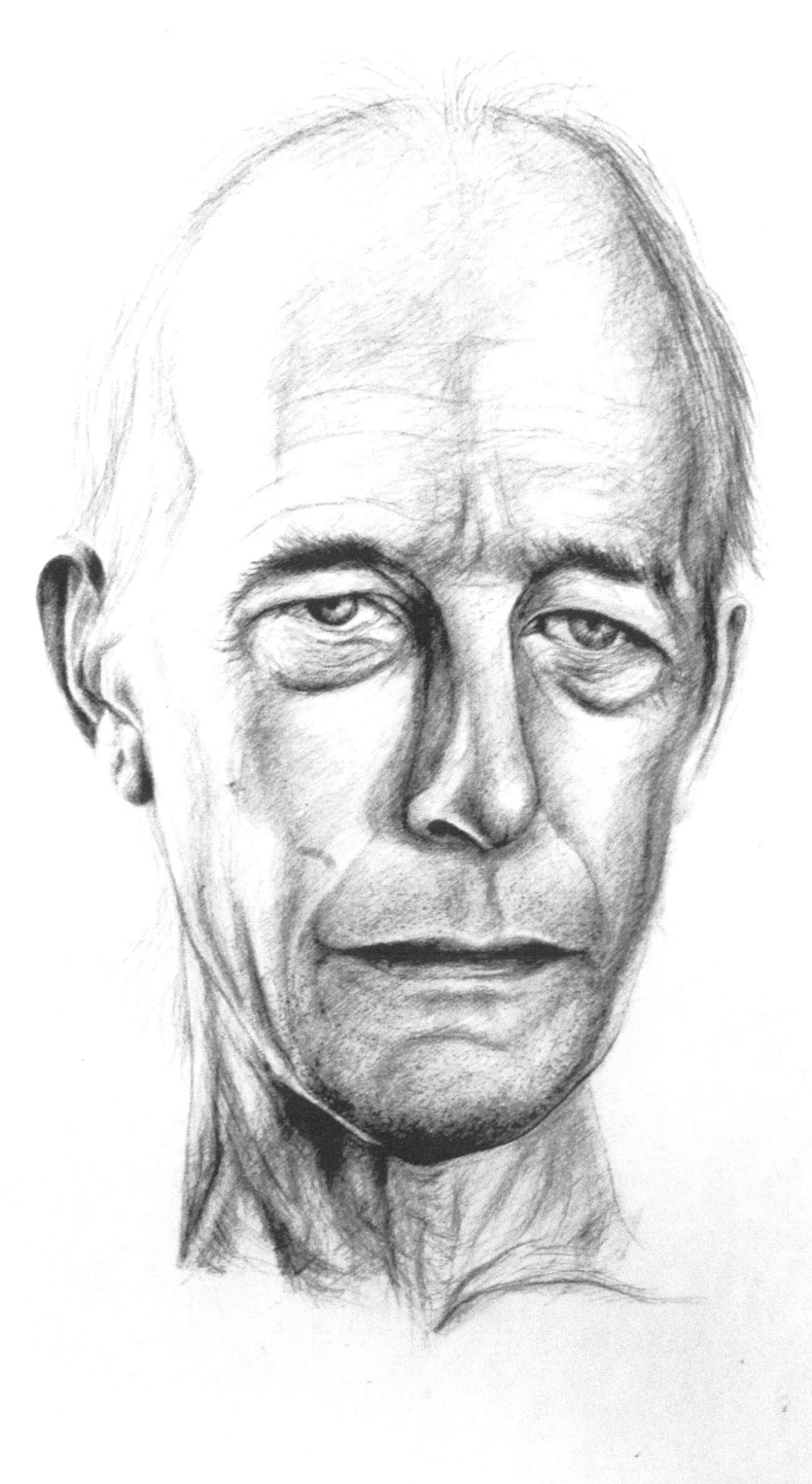

Angus, Silverpoint on prepared paper, 9" x 12", 2011

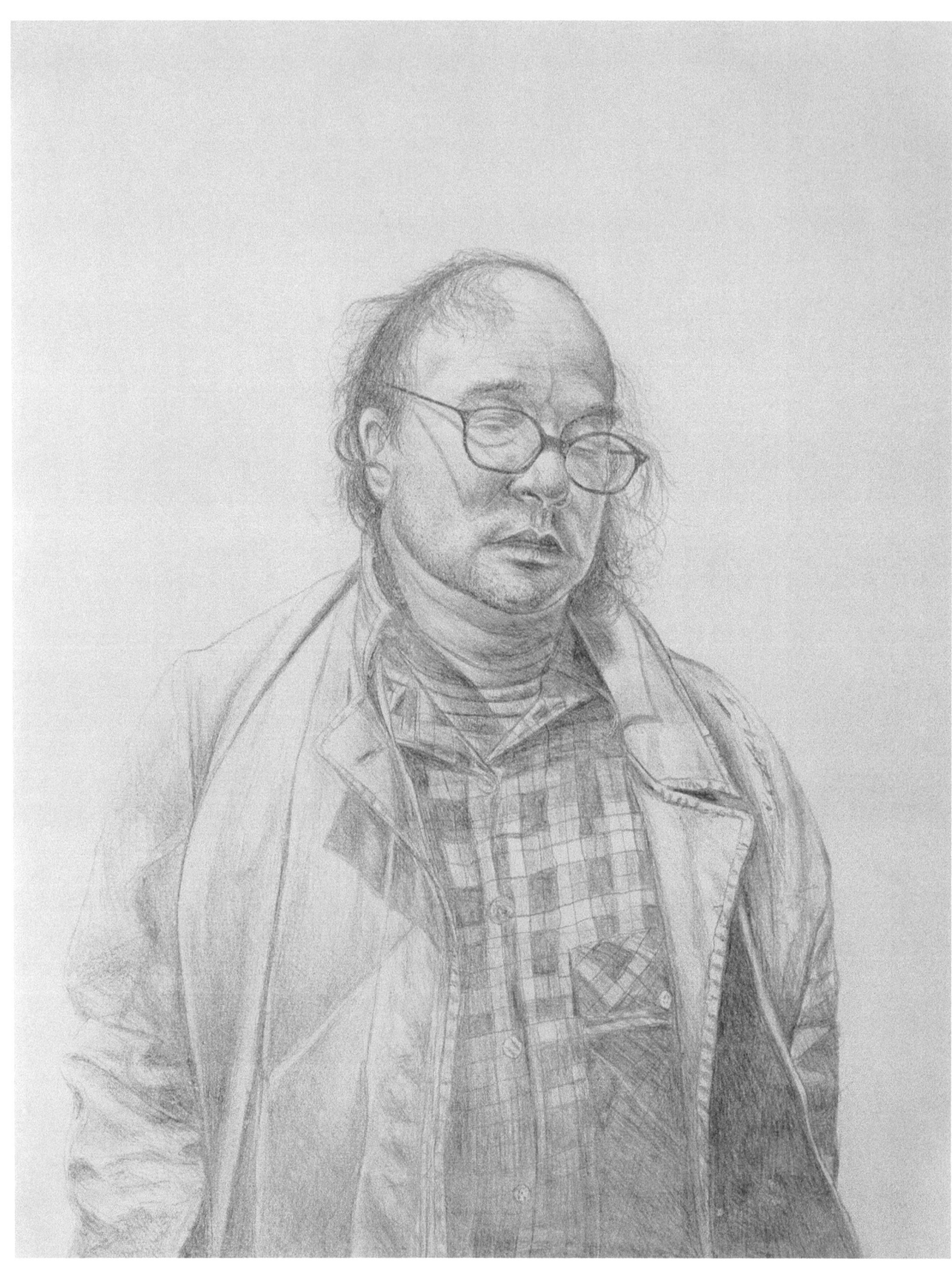

Above: Gregor, silverpoint on paper 12" x 9", 2005

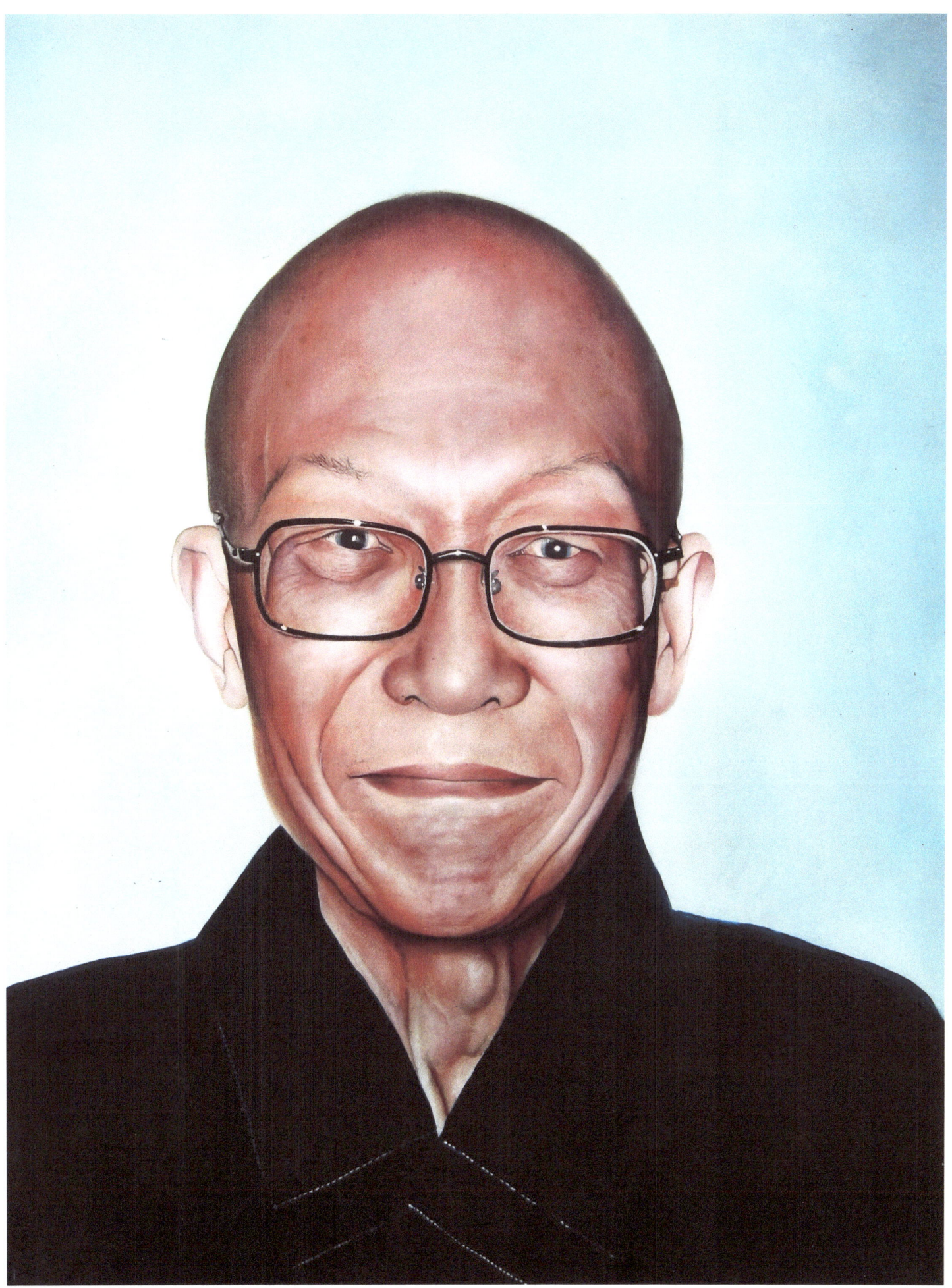

Opposite: Shifu, oil on panel, 36" x 24", 2011

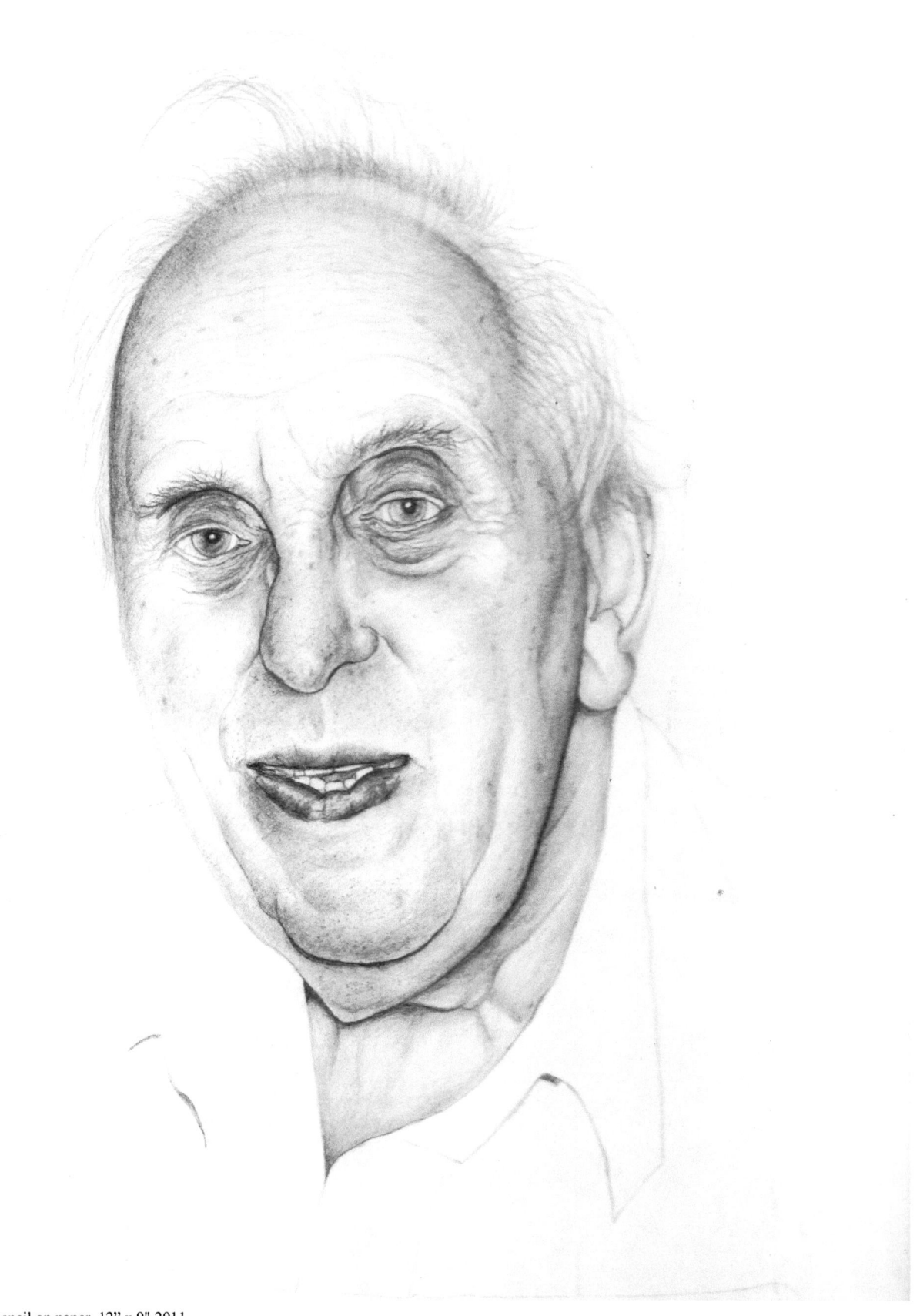

Yellop, pencil on paper, 12" x 9" 2011

GLEBOV

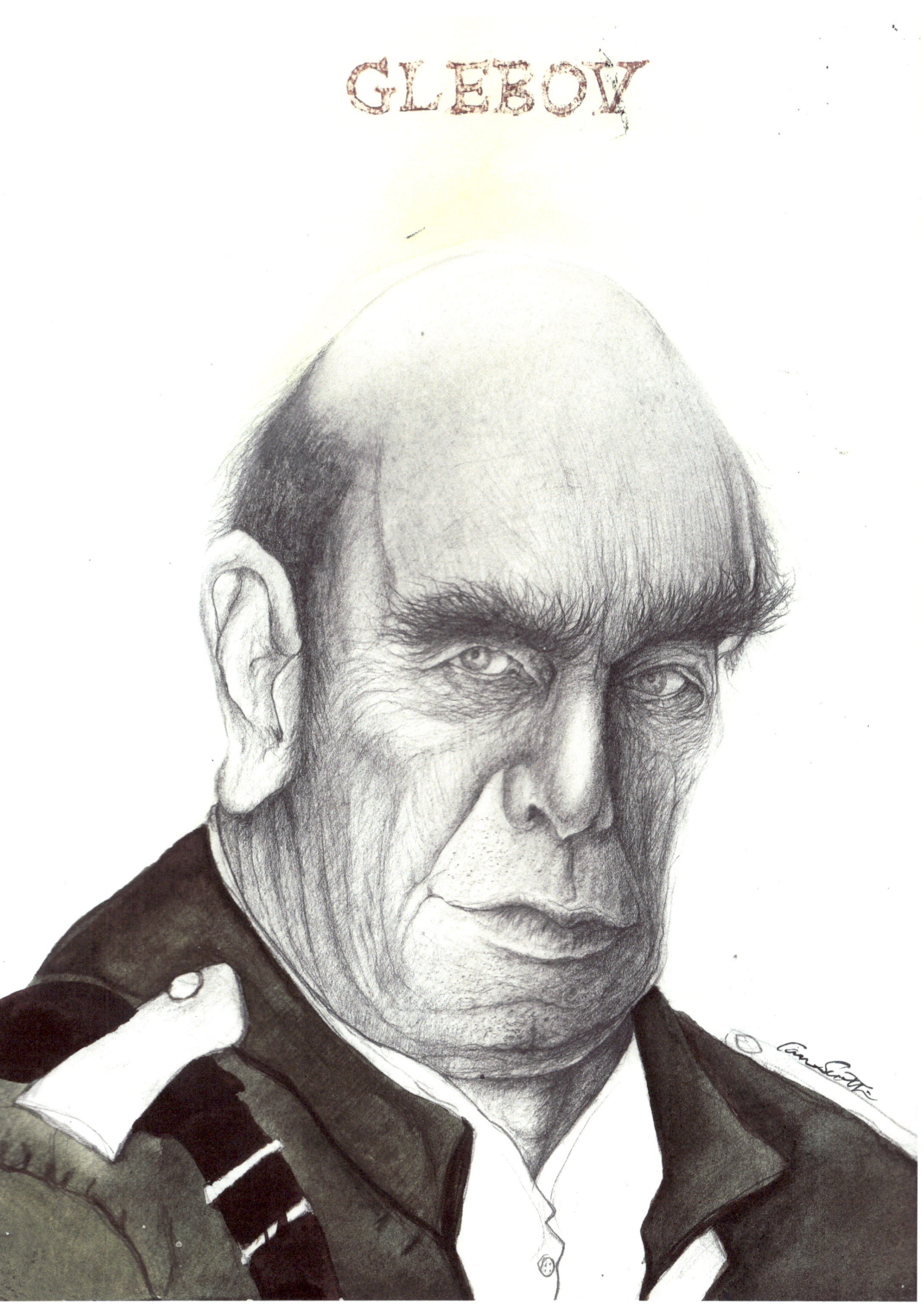

Glebov, pencil on paper, 12" x 9" 2011

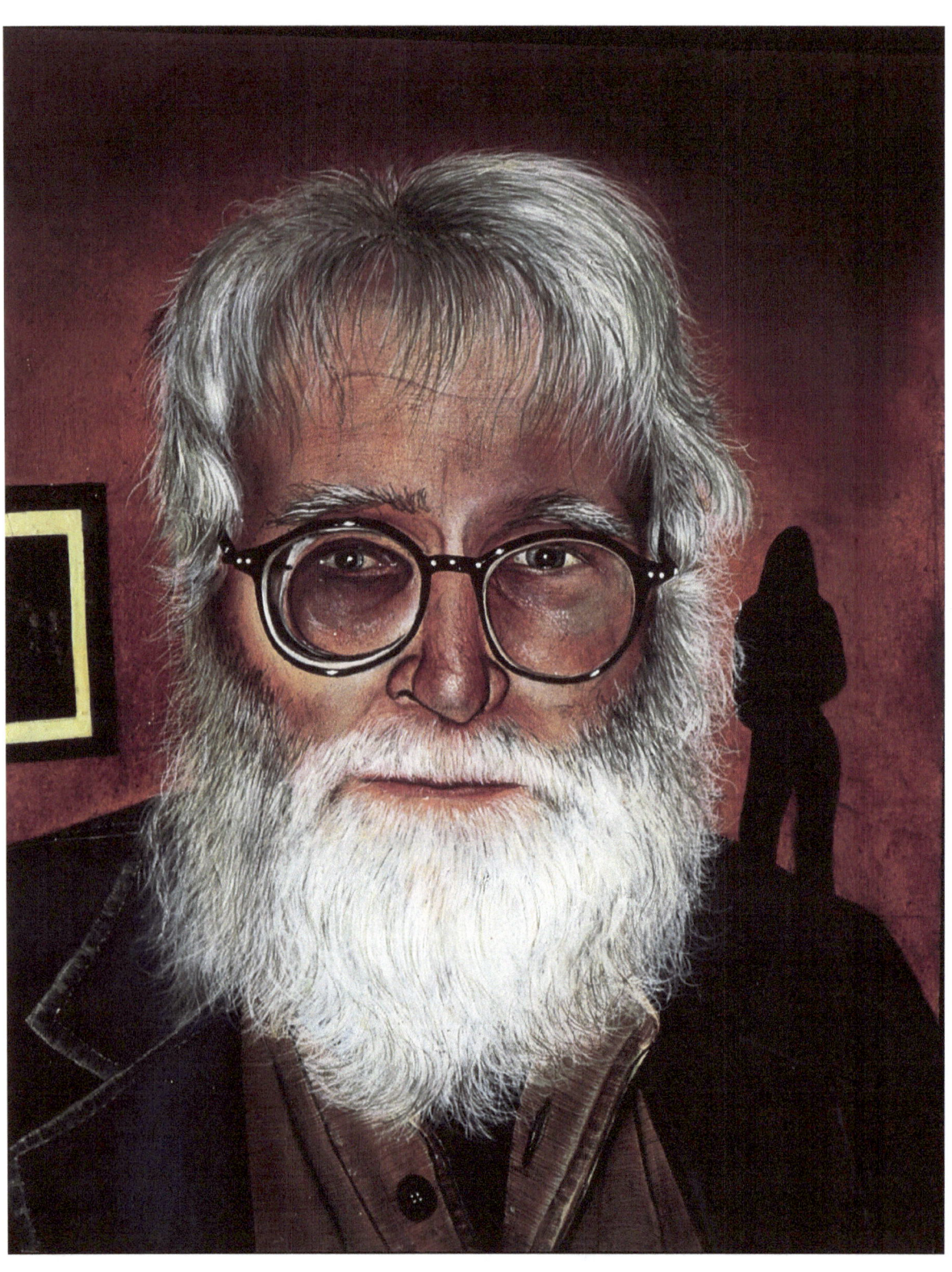

Above: Ron Kitaj, oil on wood, 10" x 8", 2005

Right: Borough Wick pencil on paper 20" x 16" 2011

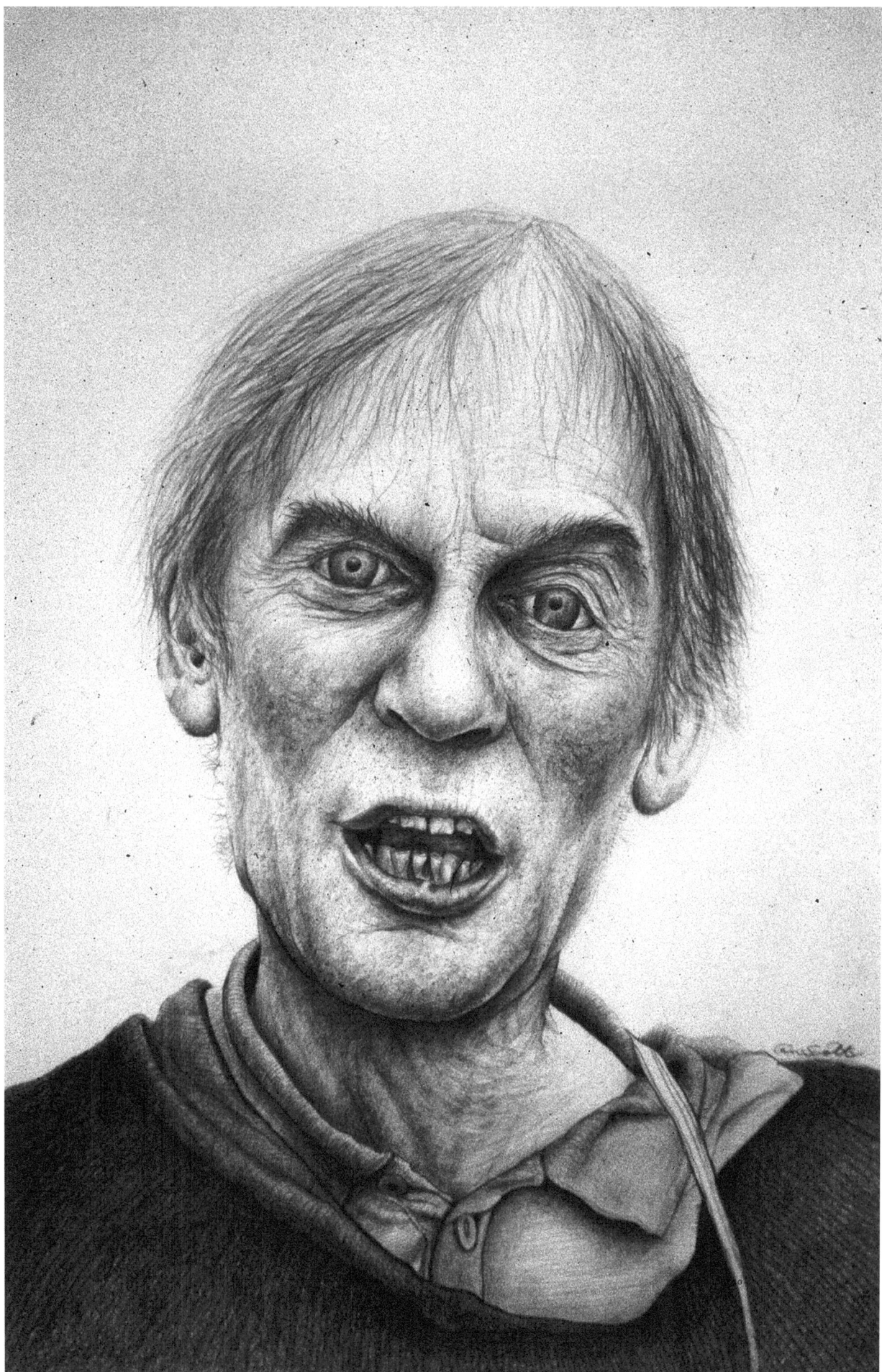

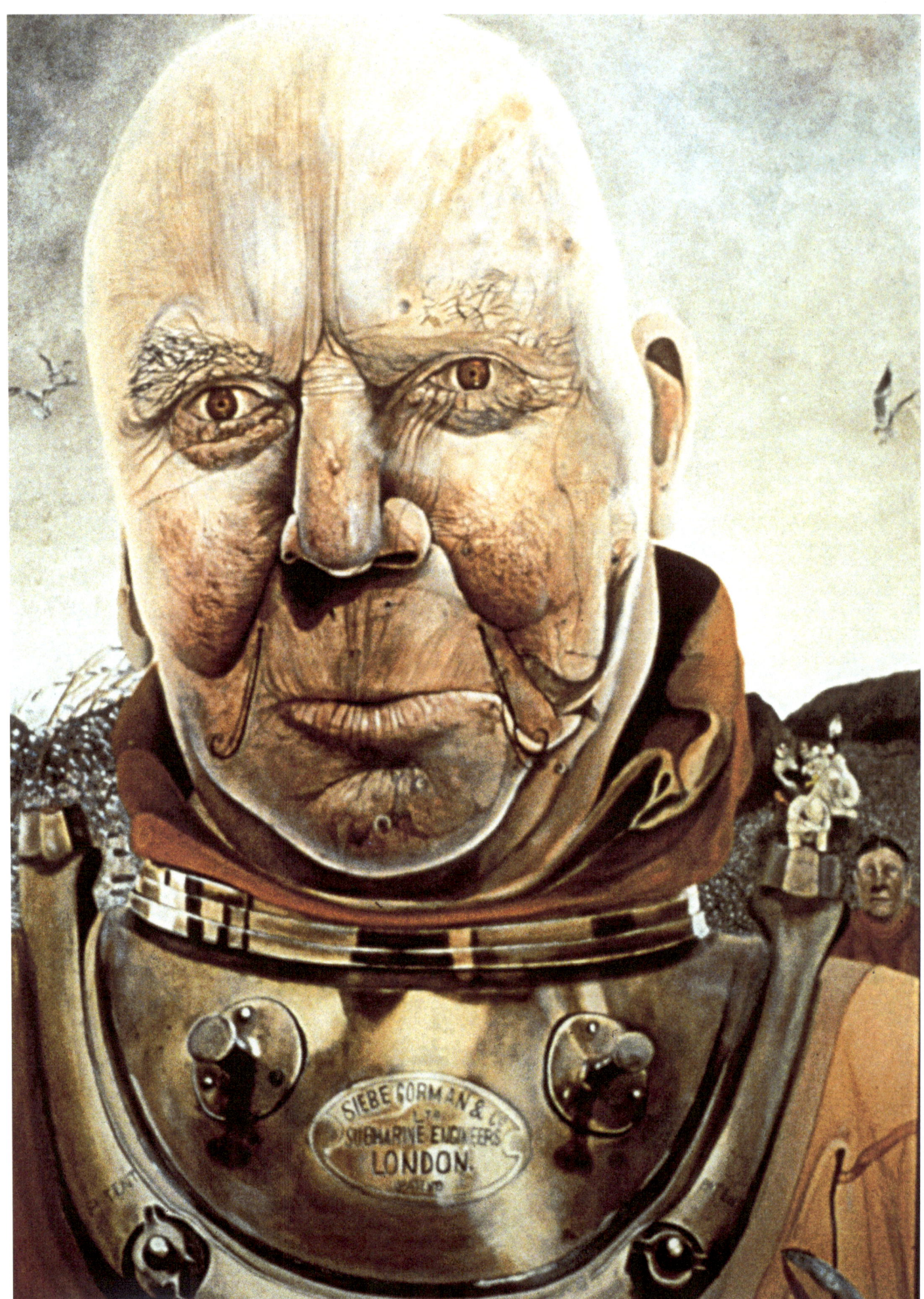

Early Large Portraits 1985- 86

Siebe Gorman, oil on wood, 72" x 48", 1986

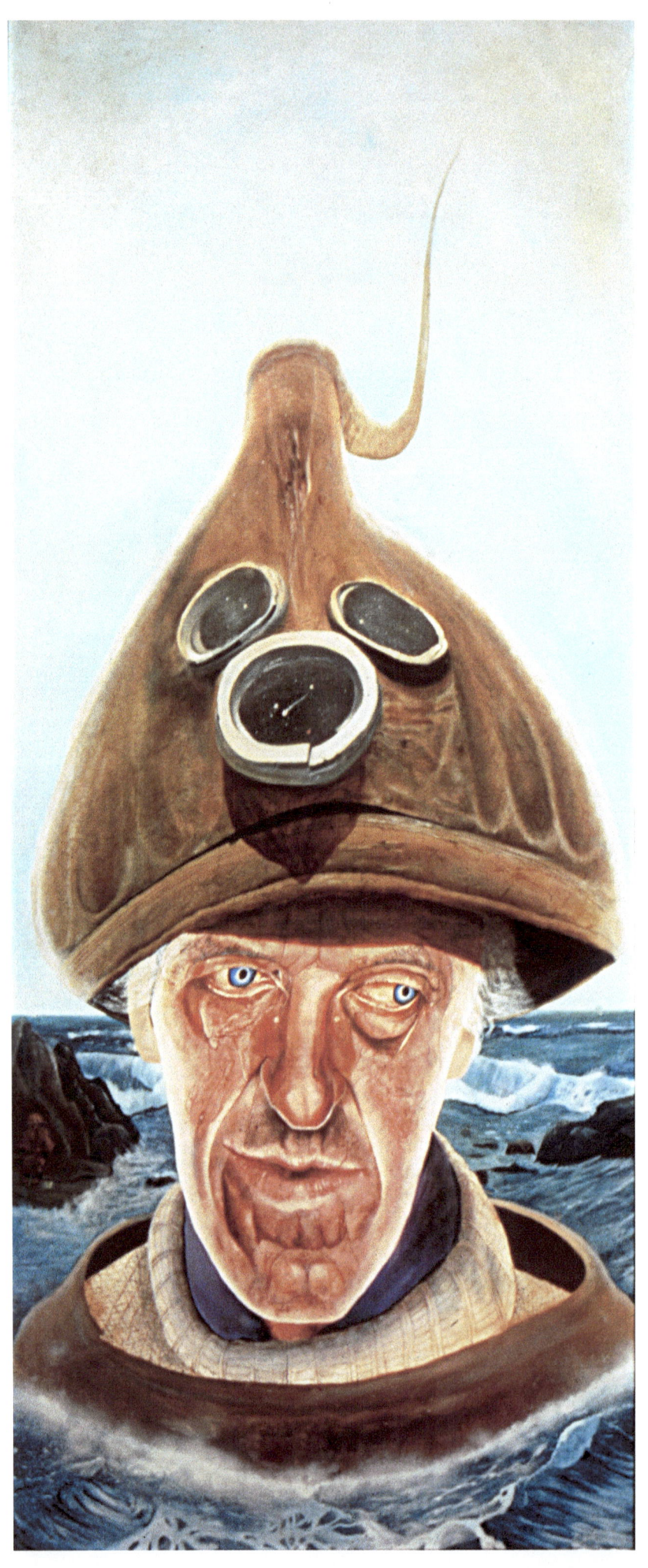

Whisper a Vow to the Long, Sweet Silence

Under Blessing and Bell

oil on wood 84" x 36" 1986

Collection of Dundee Museum and Art

Gallery

Opposite:

The Word Sea

is Small and Easily Uttered,

oil on wood

84" x 48", 1985

Collection of Dundee University

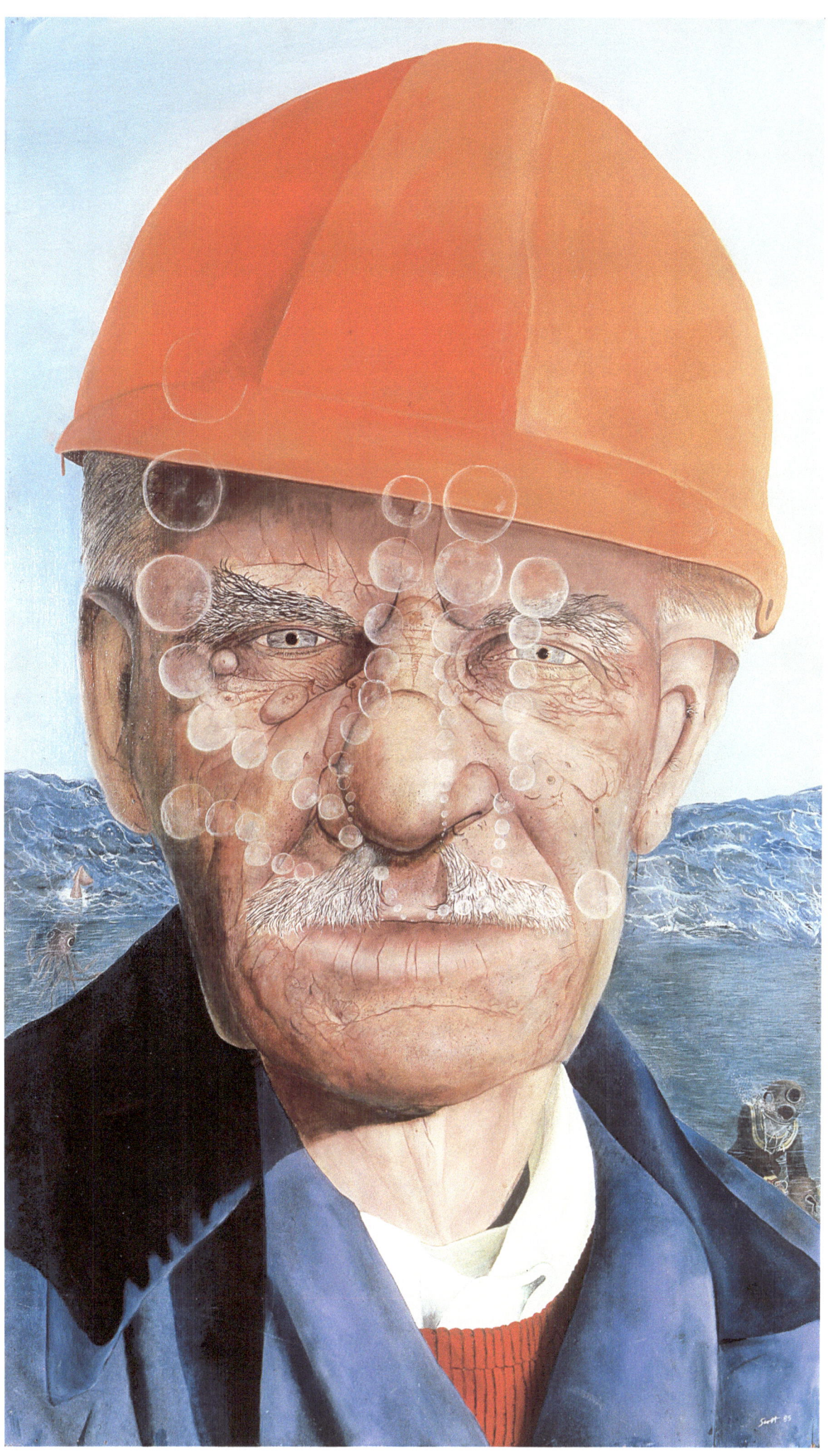

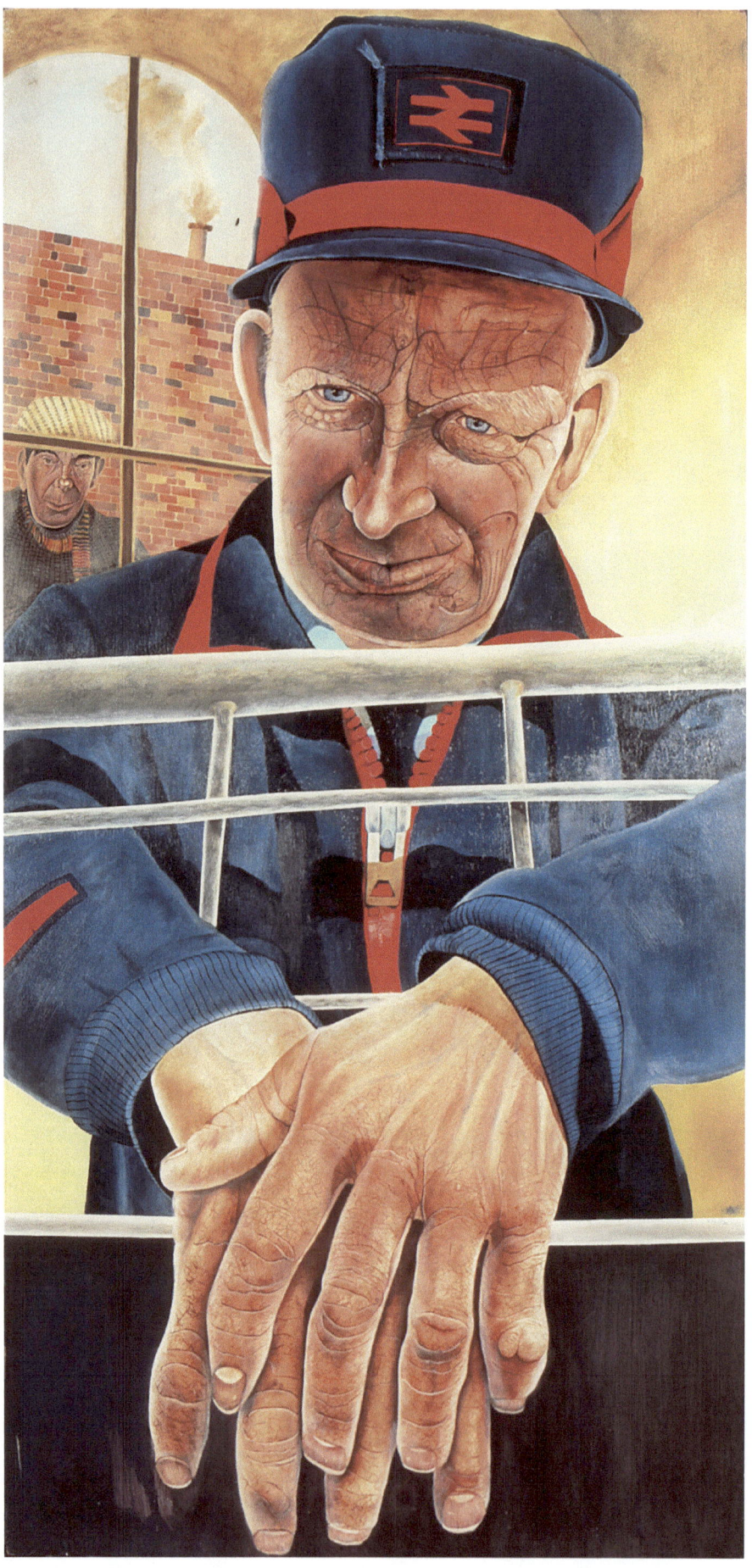

Above: On The Retirement Of John McCloud Wick Ralway Station, oil on wood, 96" x 48", 1986

Art collection Ninewells, Dundee

Opposite: Arthur Whalen, Roy Scottish Academy Cloakroom Attendent 84" x 48", 1986

Collection of Dundee University

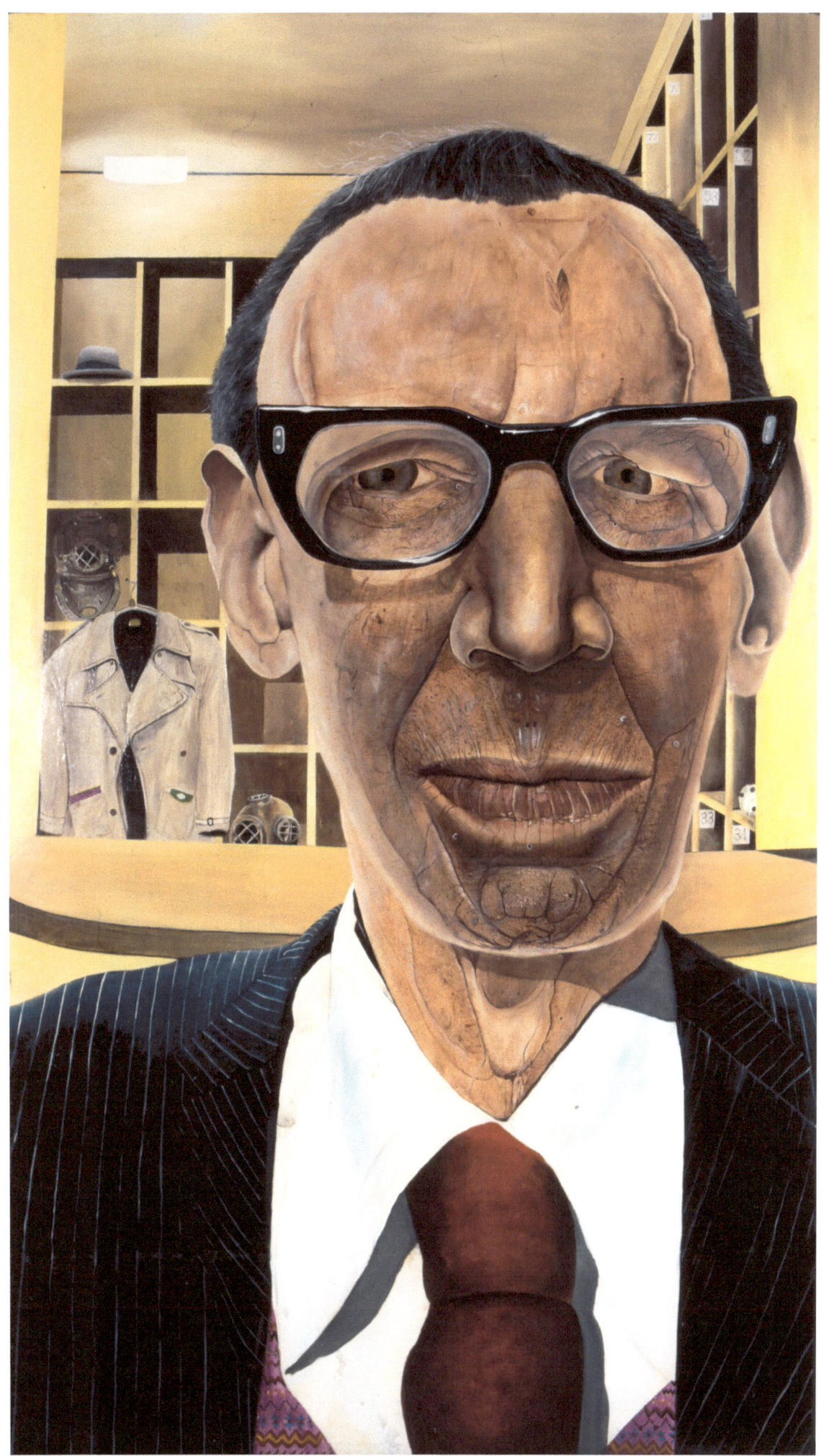

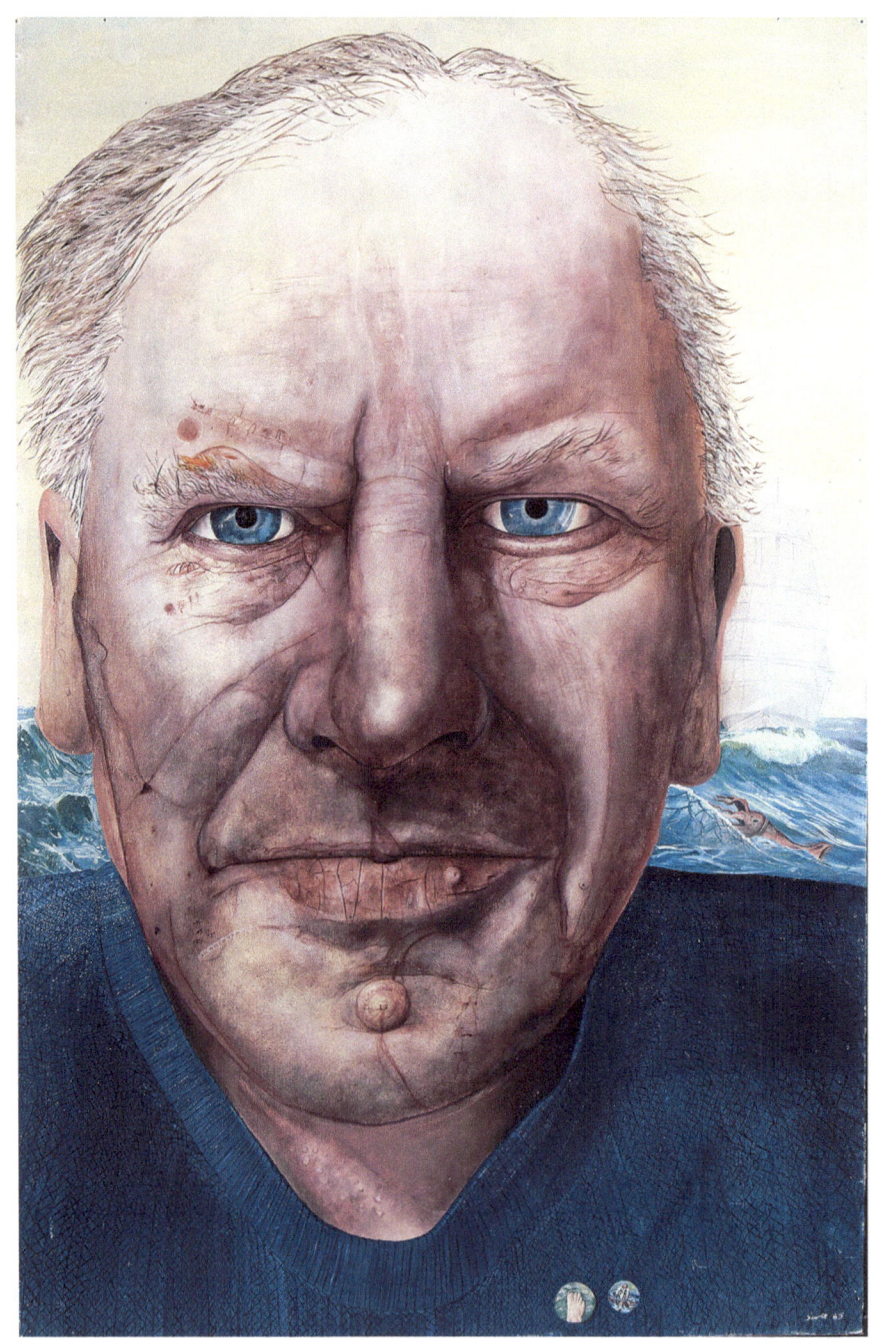

My Father oil on wood, 72" x 48", 1985

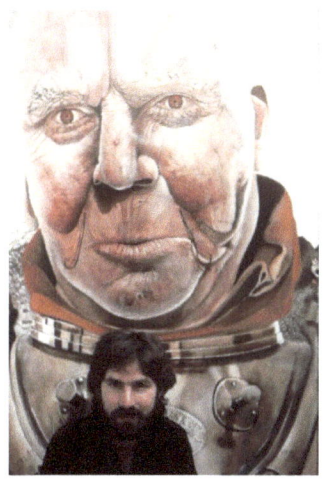

Ian Charles Scott in 1986

Ian Charles Scott comes from the remote North Highlands of Scotland. He studied film in London and worked on commercials before enrolling in Dundee University to study art. He emerged as the top student in the under and post-graduate programs there gaining a B.A. 1st class honors degree and an M.F.A. in Fine Art. Upon graduating he was immediately offered a lecturing post in Sunderland Art School. He has taught under-grad and post-graduate students for 20 years. Earlier in his career he taught an art therapy based course in a maximum-security prison.

 Ian Charles Scott is a nationally and internationally recognized artist. whose works can be found in the Scottish National Portrait Gallery, The Aberdeen Art Gallery, The Dundee Art Gallery, The Royal Scottish Academy, The Koyo Institute, and The Dublin Art Gallery, among others. In the US his works have been exhibited in the Silverstein Gallery, the Kravits Wehby Gallery, and in a touring exhibition Conversations with Jeff Koons and Frank Gehry.

He received Scotland's highest and most sought after scholarship, "The Alastair Salvasen Award" and used it to move to the United States in 1998. He started work as an adjunct at Hostos Community College in 1999 and became full-time in 2004.

To quote Hostos College-'Professor Scott has transformed the Arts curriculum at Hostos, encouraging students to explore their creativity and to contribute in countless ways to the cultural life of the Hostos community. He has a very strong following among Hostos students whom he guides and mentors in and out of the classroom.'

As an Assistant Professor in the Visual and Performing Arts Unit in the Humanities Department, he was nominated in 2009 for the New York City Mayor's Awards for Arts and Culture. The Awards acknowledge and celebrate the role individual artists, art educators, cultural organizations, corporations and philanthropists play in the public-private partnership that sustains New York City's creative vitality and economic well-being.

When referring to his nomination, Professor Scott simply states: "It's been a great honor to be nominated for the Mayor's Award."

The awards, created in 1974 by the NYC Cultural Affairs Advisory Commission, have been previously conferred to actor James Earl Jones, Composer Stephen Sondheim, playwright Tennessee Williams, musician Winton Marsalis, Nobel laureate Toni Morrison and among others, the famous American screenwriter, film director and comedian Woody Allen.

The nomination 'credits him with having transformed the college's visual arts programs along many years of complete dedication to teaching arts courses."

(Biography compiled from articles by Hostos Community College and courtesy of the college)

THE SHAPE OF THE BEING

Can a painting be an actual spiritual exploration? Will the act of making the painting have an effect of one's journey or will one's journey have an effect on the painting..?

All spiritual work in the arts unless of the most blatent materialistic existential form are vitually taboo in todays art world.

The title "THE SHAPE OF THE BEING" comes from the Koran where artists are forbidden from describing the exact shape of a living creature due to the fact one would have to then deal with the being in the afterlife.

I use the shape of the being as an excuse to allow me to meditate..the actual representation of the subject is incidental to the process. The vehicle of the paint is the allow a meditation on the nature of being to take place..Is there a direct connection between us and the spiritual universe my conclusions are yes..every move we make and discovery we make has a direct consequence in the development of human collective spirit.

The artworld of dealers and auction houses with the curatorial system of heirachy has resulted in a world drained of arts possibility of transformation. We are left with a hollow creation that does not fufill the great possibility of creativity.

The removal of the spiritual significance of art and it's replacement with only the materialistic significance is being slowly redressed by a dedicated band of pioneers.

What ever their angle, whether it be religious, esoteric or occult they are returning art to it's driver's seat in the transformative potential of humankind.

Right now we are on the pivot of stasis. A stasis where the most publicised and expensive art is the most cynical and in many cases not touched by the artist but produced by a factory of lowly paid employee's under the "masters name".

This is a dreadful subversion of Remberandts workshop into the methodology of Henry Ford.

I feel by active contemplation of my works an opening into the transformative potentials will open up as it has for me and through this tiny chink of light we will illuminate the "Plato's Cave" and allow consciousness to wake up.

Professor Ian Charles Scott

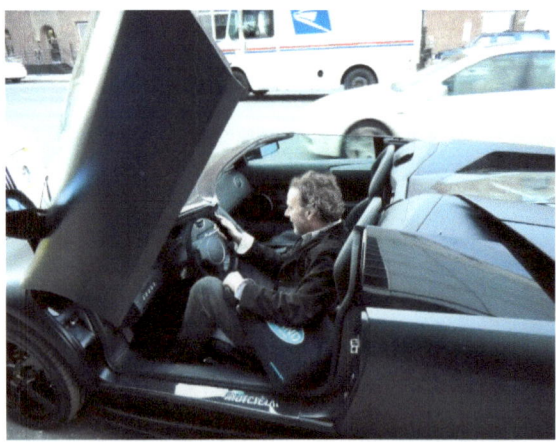

Opposite: " The Volume of Being" oil on Panel 8" x 8" 2014

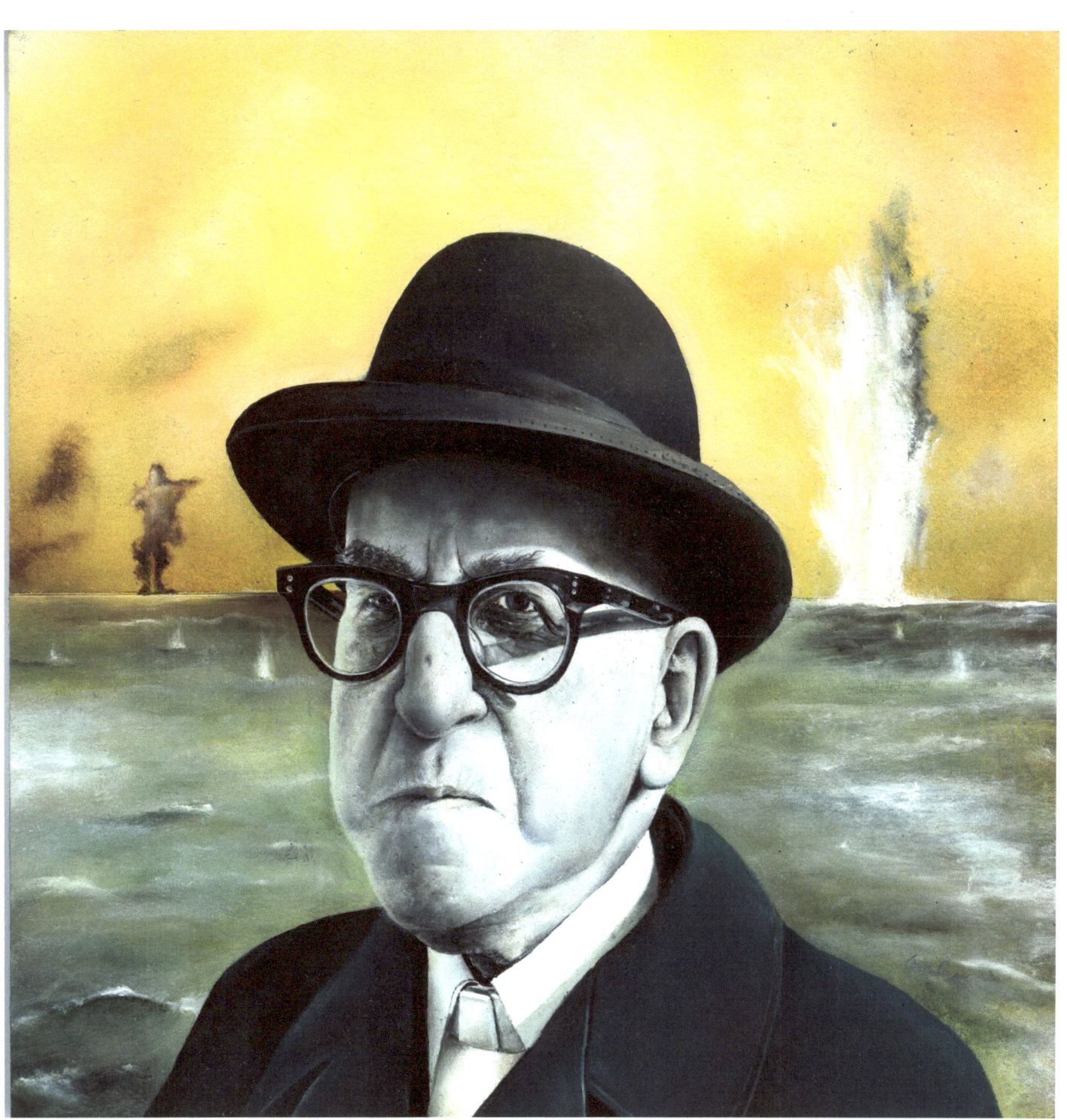

VICTORY HALL PRESS

is a division of Victory Hall Inc.,

a not-for-profit arts organization producing exhibitions, events,

education programs, public projects and publications,

based in the NJ/NY metro area.

Other books include:

PORTRAIT PROJECT

Ross Bonn:100 People

NEW DRAWING SERIES

presents series of innovative, current images

from artists whose work explores and expands

the visual and conceptual language of drawing.

Ibou Ndoye: Forms of Faces

Ibou Ndoye: Taarou Adaa

Jill Scipione: Skullnotebook

Carl Vierow: Detective at Red Castle Pier and Other Drawings

James Pustorino: Universechild

Hector G Romero: Last Coast Blues

To order copies : victoryhallpress.org

Victory Hall Inc. 74 W 46 St

Bayonne, NJ 07002

www.victoryhall.org

August 2014

Victory Hall Press

ISBN-13: 978-0692254349

ISBN-10: 069225434X

Copyright © 2014

Editor: James Pustorino

website: www.victoryhallpress.org

contact: victoryhall1@msn.com

This program is made possible in part by funds from the New Jersey State Council on
the Arts/Department of State, a partner agency of the National Endowment for the Arts, administered by the Hudson County Office of
Cultural and Heritage Affairs, Thomas A. Degise, County Executive, and the Board of Chosen Freeholders.

Opposite: George Mackay Brown, 12" x 9" pencil 1995

Overleaf: In the Sun's Last House, oil on canvas 30" x 20", 1996

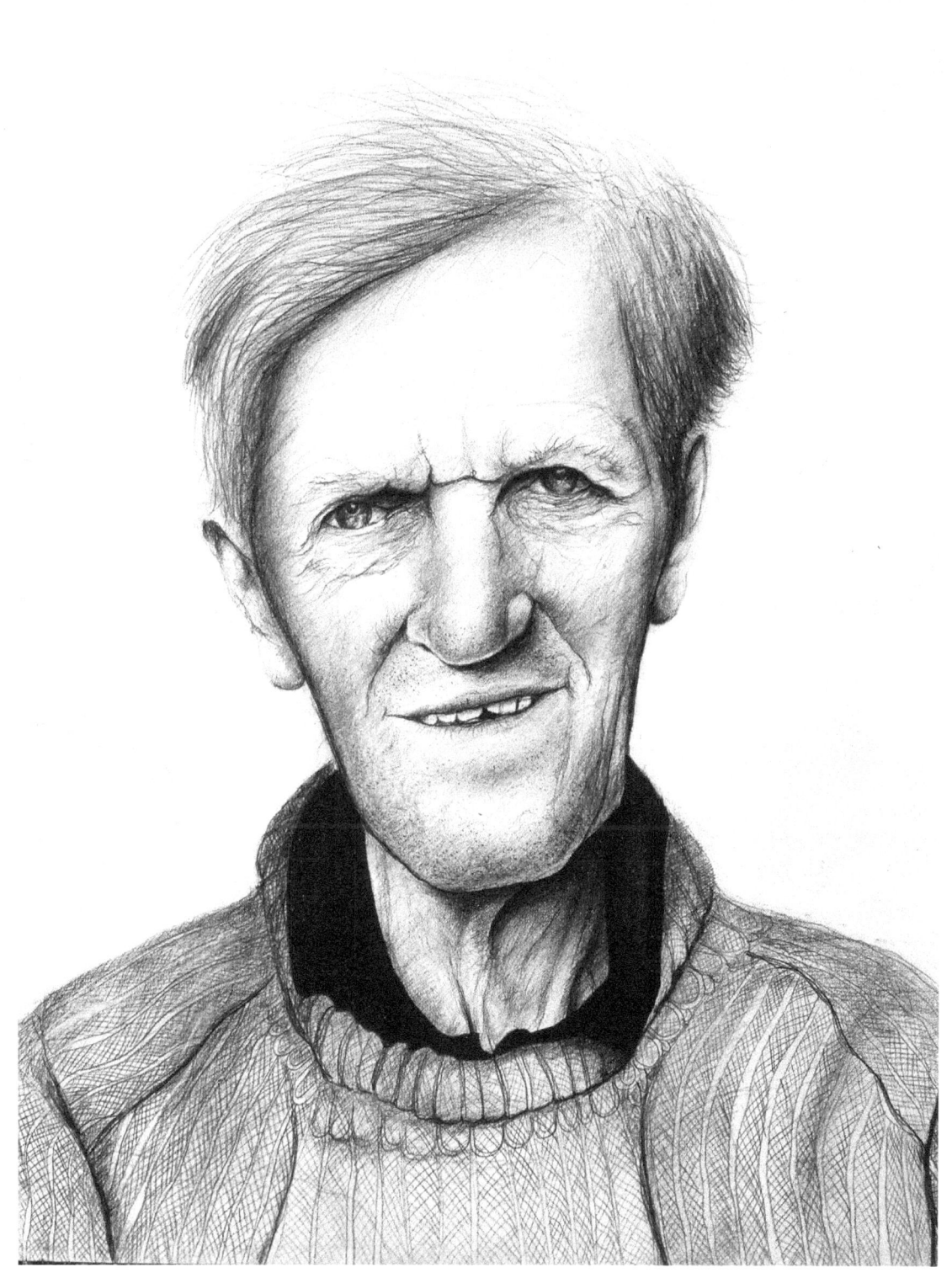

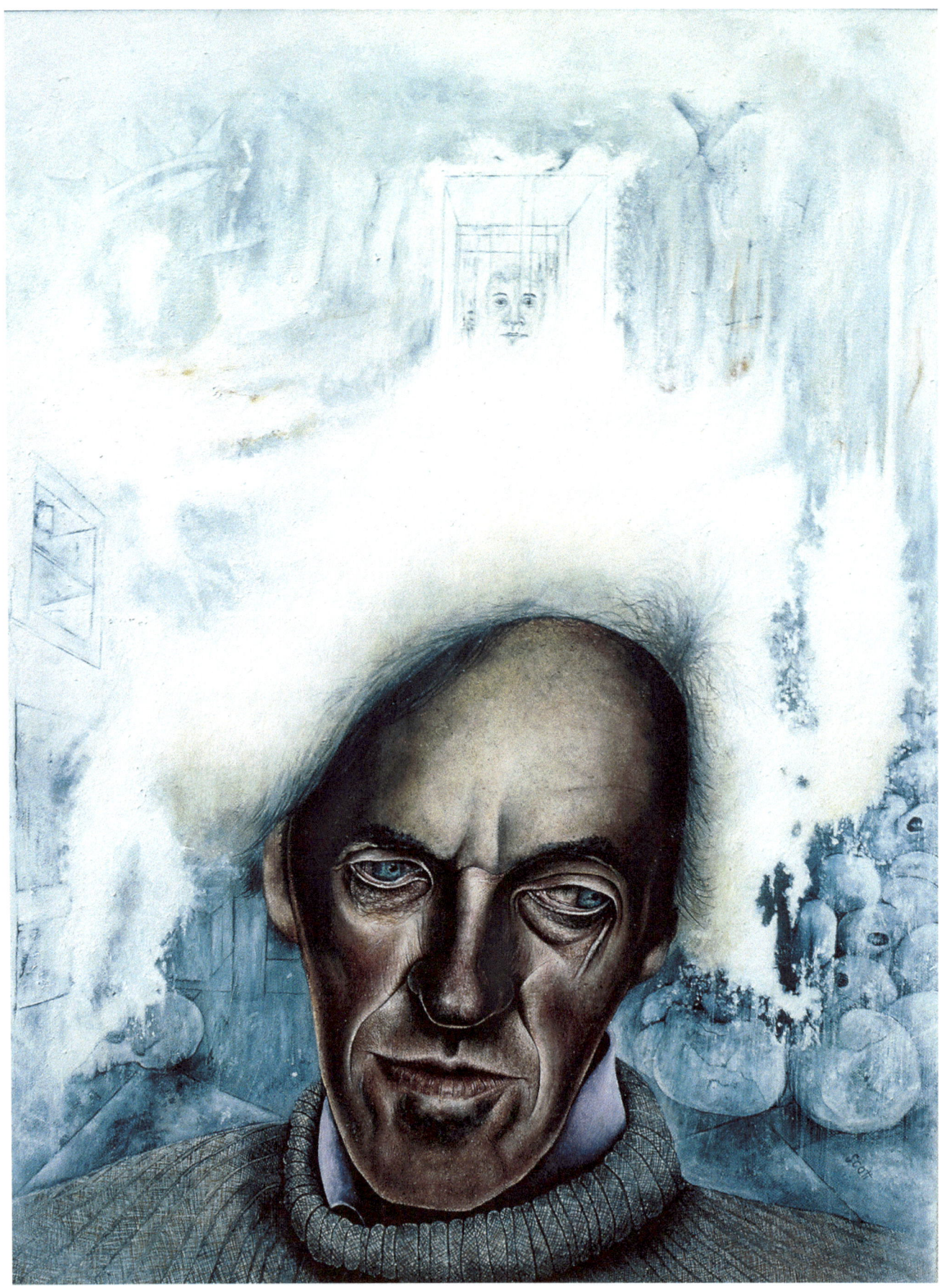